SHADOWFALL

Reflections on Nurturing Family Values

A. GAIL SMITH

Deseret Book Company
Salt Lake City, Utah

To my children
Glenna, Stacie, Sharwan, Joseph, Rebecca, and Jacob

And in memory of
Shilo Sharwan and Abby Gail

ISBN 1-57345-145-2

Printed in the United States of America

10   9   8   7   6   5   4   3   2   1

Contents

Acknowledgments

In 1987, when I first began to put down on paper the thoughts and experiences that resulted in this book, I had no notion that it would take so long or that it would involve the efforts of so many people.

During those eight years, the realities of mortal life have helped focus my thinking and provided unanticipated testing of the ideas I have tried to organize and express. As difficult and soul-wrenching as some of those tests have been, they have made me even more certain that I was dealing with true principles that were worth sharing with others. I thank my Heavenly Father for that assurance.

As the book evolved, I quickly realized that I could not do it alone. I have been amazed at the way that different people just seemed to come along at the right time to help me clarify my thinking, bring greater unity to the narrative, and, occasionally, to get me back on track.

Jenny Miller Higby, a high school friend of my eldest daughter, Glenna, and a family friend ever since, has sat at the computer across the table from me for hours at a stretch, using her training in literature, English, and grammar to help me put my thoughts into intelligible sentences with words, phrases, and punctuation marks in the right places. Her dedication to the task, even through pregnancy and a move to Idaho, are deeply appreciated.

I would also like to thank Jerry Pulsipher, who drew upon his own roots in and love of Utah's Dixie to add historical and descriptive touches. Jerry was also invaluable in bringing out many of the deeper principles at work in the story, and in making the transitions in the narrative flow more smoothly.

Lavina Fielding Anderson, who read the manuscript in its early stages, demonstrated great patience with a novice author. She showed an uncanny ability in motivating me to reach deep within and clearly identify the underlying structure that made the book hang together as more than a collection of stories. Her encouragement that I was on the right track and her careful editing for style and consistency were most appreciated.

Also, I have appreciated the support and help of Lowell M. Durham Jr. and of the publishing staff at Deseret Book. They sensed intuitively what I was trying to do with the book and have brought it to final fruition with professionalism and understanding.

There are so many others who have contributed—friends and relatives who have pushed me along, been excited about the stories, and encouraged me at times when I needed to know that the book could fill an important need. You know who you are. All I can say is thanks.

Finally, I express gratitude for my family, from whom my greatest strength and support has come. Without them, there would have been no book to write.

Throughout our life together, my husband, Hyrum, has shown an incredible willingness to risk his money and his talent and his time to ensure that his family was loved, cared for, protected, and taught righteous principles. His encouragement to see this book through to completion has been a major source of my own strength. We have truly been equally yoked in the larger effort of trying to bring a family through the mortal stage of eternal life.

And then there are my children—Glenna, Stacie, Sharwan, Joseph, Rebecca, and Jacob. They have each, in turn, received what we were trying to pass on to them, that which is precious and good from those who have gone before them in the eternal family. With joy I have watched them begin their own transfer of these things to their children. I cannot thank them enough for making this mother's life easier by being the receptive and stalwart spirits they are.

Last and most important of all, I want to acknowledge the ongoing eternal process that this book attempts to describe—the accumulating heritage that has come to us from our ancestors and that, with the contribution we add, will be passed forward to those who come after. I thank my great-grandparents and grandparents and parents for their teachings, for their dedication, for their commitment to family life. I only hope our generation and our children's generation can do as well in passing on that priceless treasure.

The Shadowfall

SHIRLEY M. HOWARD

Once earth
Called to me,
"Be a tree,
Be a tree."
Acorn—I answered
With a leaf,
A stem,
And a brief
Root shooting down;
Sending a young trunk
Bending in the wind,
And a
New limb strong
Enough for just a bird
And a song.

Now I
Have heard
A thousand songs,
Stirred
In a thousand winds
And a
Thousand leaves
Weave
Through my
Branches.
My roots
Lie deep
And I keep
Thinking
That when
One is tall
The shadowfall
Is long
Upon
An afternoon

Prologue: Be a tree

I don't know why I connected with "The Shadowfall" when I first discovered the poem as a seventeen-year-old growing up in rural America during the 1950s. I read it in the *Relief Society Magazine*, to which my mother subscribed because she loved the faith-promoting stories, historical vignettes, and poetry. The poem was overprinted on a gigantic leafy oak tree, towering protectively over a well-traveled lane that led off into the unseen distance.

I didn't see my first real oak tree until I was twenty-one, serving as a Mormon missionary in England. Those majestic trees were in direct contrast with the oaks I was used to: scrub oak that fought mesquite and juniper, inch by inch, for each pocket of soil on the red hills of southern Utah's Dixie. They were tough, tangled, shrubby things with sharp, resilient twigs that would bend, twist, and contort but wouldn't break. The bark was rough and so were the branches. Scrub oaks could draw blood as fast as the country's bristling Joshua trees.

Despite my lack of personal experience with the stately oak tree described in it, the poem stirred something within me. Recognition. A connection with my heritage. I knew what deep roots meant, and strength, endurance, and the influence that stretches protectively yet commandingly from one generation into the next. I had heard the call, "Be a tree."

I have not been able to find out much about Shirley M. Howard, the author of the poem, or where she grew up that she answered "oak." I would have answered "cottonwood," perhaps because of the country lane, lined with gigantic cottonwood trees, that began just below Grandma Cooper's house and ended a quarter-mile away at the creek bottom. I drove our milk cows to pasture each morning and back each evening to the corrals. That heavily shaded piece of the journey kept this small cowherder cool during the hot summer day—as it had my father years earlier on the same trek.

The call "Be a tree" also reminded me of the ancient ash tree with the trumpet vine clinging and climbing around its rotund trunk until the vine disappeared high up, enveloped inside the leafy branches. Planted with care and often hand watered by Great-Grandmother Averett, the ash was stationed magnificently in front of our house, bespeaking dignity, endurance, and the enormous patience exercised by the shade-starved pioneers. The two mulberry trees behind our house were great, green survivors of an 1870 experiment in pioneer Utah silk production. When autumn filled the air, those two trees hosted flocks of chirping English sparrows, reminding me that migratory creatures—birds as well as people—still have unchanging places of refuge.

Those trees of antiquity seemed to connect me with my Dixie roots—roots that ran deep, supporting enormous, strong trunks and branches sprawling outward and upward. For this reason, the vivid tree imagery portrayed by "The Shadowfall" rang true to my spirit. It connected me with my past, but when I read it I also saw myself as the new acorn with the ability to branch out in any direction.

Thirty-five years later, as I write from our home in St. George, Utah, I see out my window the sharply white Mormon temple and the red sandstone tabernacle—both monuments to the pioneer spirit that tamed this harsh country. From this view I also see myriad trees: cottonwood, ash, mulberry, pecan, willow, fig, and pomegranate—five generations' worth of plantings now, starkly green against the red earth that sustains them. I am currently in the "shadowfall" stage of life. I have come full circle, and while traveling that circle, I have learned that there are many ways of being a tree.

I often think about the cultural changes and differences in family life between my parents' generation, my own, and that of my children. Those three generations span a period that has witnessed some of the greatest cultural change in recorded history—from horsepower and manual labor to laser power and robotic manufacturing. My parents, although living and rearing a family in the post-World War II era, were products of the last stages of rural, nineteenth-century America, with its reliance on hard work, self-sufficiency, community caring, and a strongly knit nuclear and extended family.

When I was growing up, circumstances required my family to be disciplined simply in order to survive. It was natural for us all, from age six to ninety-six, to work hard. We had to rise early just to get the morning fire going and the house warm. Even breakfast was an hour's operation. My mother, with my sisters' help, would make homemade biscuits and gravy or bacon and eggs; even oatmeal required twenty minutes to cook in those days. While they made breakfast and did the household chores, Dad and I would go out to get all the farm chores done before going to work or school.

I was fourteen years old before the first television came to our town. All the kids in the neighborhood crowded in to see the Nisson family's novelty: a huge black box, complete with an elaborate, twenty-foot antenna. When stabilized on their rooftop with guy wires, the monstrous antenna enabled them to get three channels of snowy black-and-white reception.

The first TV program I watched all the way through was during the Thanksgiving holiday at Granny Wilkins's house in Salt Lake City. I still remember lying on my stomach on the floor amid my cousins as we watched a cowboy show—most likely featuring Roy Rogers, my childhood hero—complete with a sheriff's posse chasing the bank robbers, their pistols firing wildly into the air.

At that time, we Dixie folks received news about the "outside world" in one of three ways: by listening to the radio, reading the two-day-old *Salt Lake Tribune*, or watching the Movietone newsreels before the main feature at the movie house. Communications in general were much slower. My kids can't imagine the antiquated telephone system I describe to them. Those were the days of the black, boxy, no-dialing-mechanism phones. When you wanted to place a call, you lifted the receiver, waited for the operator to ask, "Number, please," and listened to her ring the number you requested. Ten families shared our party line: 790J 1 through 5 and 790R 1 through 5. Though we couldn't hear the rings of the five "R" families, we could hear their conversations if they were speaking when we picked up the phone. Because all the "J" lines rang on our phone, each family had a designated ringing signal: ours was one long, one short. Everybody knew each family's ring; when we heard one long and two short, we knew the phones would be in use for a long time. May, who lived down the street, would be calling her sister-in-law Mina with the latest news.

Though there was a strict code of respect for telephone privacy, once in a while, if I picked up the phone to call a friend, I might accidentally overhear May say to Mina, "Did you hear about Delores?" My natural instinct made me want to listen in, but my conscience and respect for the "code" made me put the receiver back down. Their conversation might delay my phone call for an hour or more, but that was the way of life. There was no real urgency.

For today's children, there is no waiting. To share a party line is unthinkable. Our advanced communications systems include call waiting, voice messaging, portable cellular phones, teleconferencing, fax machines, and satellite broadcasts. We live in an age of instant food, instant communication, instant gratification, work-saving household devices—and disintegrating families.

Modern conveniences have eliminated much of the drudgery of family life and have increased the opportunities for leisure pursuits. But at the same time, they have taken away the natural childhood learning opportunities that taught me the work ethic, creativity, traditional values, and the importance of paying the price to reach a lofty dream or worthy goal. And they have contributed to the negative media influences our society experiences. Viewing today's television and movie offerings, is it any wonder that too many people seem to be overly self-centered, have poor interpersonal communication, or show lack of commitment to almost anything, including the challenges of making marriages or family relationships work?

I'm grateful for the commitment to marriage and family that was modeled by my parents. It has shone as an example in my own married life. My husband, Hyrum, and I met in England when we were both serving there as Mormon missionaries. I still marvel at the manner of our meeting, but that's getting ahead of the story. As to our life together, no image of trees, rooted in place, can describe the whirlwind of events that led us to the point at which we now find ourselves. If Hyrum had been a rancher, I would have bucked hay bales beside him. If he had been a farmer, I would have shouldered a shovel and walked the irrigation ditches with him. But Hyrum's talents lie in teaching and motivating and marketing, often in jobs as a manager or executive. So I've been an executive's wife. It seems we have always been in motion: St. George, Oklahoma, Germany, and Brigham Young University; then on to Hawaii, Oregon, California, back to northern Utah, and finally home to St. George. We averaged four years in each place.

In 1983, what is now the Franklin Quest Company was conceived in the basement of our home, with the creation of H. W. Smith and Associates. At that point I was mother, wife, secretary, accountant, seminar registrar, logistics operator, manual collator of seminar materials (with the children's help), and anything that had to do with setting up and closing down a seminar. Hyrum marketed and taught the seminars. A short time later came the Franklin Day

Planner, the time-management tool at the heart of the training seminars, and I opened and operated the first Franklin store. As the company grew, others took over the responsibilities the children and I had helped pioneer, and I resumed my full-time focus on my family.

As a result of the success of the company and Hyrum's skill at teaching and motivating people, we have spent most of our married life in the public eye. However, the secret heart of our life together has always been our marriage and family, and it is there that both Hyrum and I have experienced our deepest inner fulfillment.

This book is about that secret heart, about the challenges as well as the enormous untold joy of healthy family life, in both the good times and the not so good. It is about the quiet, deliberate ways one family sought to create, nurture, and transfer that joy from shadowfall to shadowfall.

Over the last few years, many in America have expressed increasing concern about the state of the family unit. In this reawakening, there is growing alarm about the failure of such substitutes for the traditional family as street gangs, communes, and inadequate day-care centers. Many wring their hands over mounting statistics of divorce, child sexual abuse, and illiteracy, and different programs are put forward to cure or alleviate these ills among parents and children. While I share deeply the concerns about where the American family finds itself today, I believe that our best hope for combatting such problems lies in *prevention*—the kind of prevention that begins and has the greatest chance of taking root in the childhood years.

Looking back on my own life, I realize that there were many magical moments and hours when I was taught (without knowing that I was being taught) the important lessons of life. Seen in retrospect, those lessons are the greatest legacy bequeathed to me by my parents: treasured values about the things that matter most, like the necessity for and satisfactions of working hard, caring for others, taking responsibility for one's actions, getting an education, and appreciating life's spiritual side. I realize now that my family's daily schedule during my childhood, though we lived that way purely out of necessity, actually provided a natural learning time that no longer exists for most families.

When Hyrum and I were first married, we recognized that the world we had grown up in was vastly different from the world in which we would be raising our children. We knew we would have to consciously create many of the learning experiences that had sprung naturally from the environment in our generation. In these pages I am hoping to share what we have learned in our own family's quest. I am sending a gentle message to young men and young women in the early stages of family formation—or even before marriage—but also to married couples, single parents, teachers, grandparents, and anyone who cares about today's children: "Plant acorns; think roots; shape branches; be a tree."

This book is not a how-to parenting book, although it contains many how-to suggestions. It does not provide tips and programs to help entice teens home from malls and video arcades, although it does describe some of what our own children were doing at that age and why. It's not about household and time management, although our life and family needs have required both.

This book is about family relationships, about discipline and miracles and the deep roots of loving and living by principles and values. It's about the magical years of childhood and the long shadowfall of parental influence.

1

Once earth called to me

One of our enduring family memories is of Hyrum surveying our six-year-old Glenna approvingly just after she had straightened out a crumpled rug before walking over it—a distinctly Hyrum-like thing to do. Hyrum announced proudly, "Glenna, you have my genes."

"Oh, no, I don't," she retorted. "Your jeans are too big!"

I'm truly fascinated by what scientists are discovering about genetic inheritance and the subtle ways it interacts with environment and nurture in shaping character, defining goals, and confirming talents. It causes me to think about my own inheritance. How much comes from Dixie genes passed down to me from my ancestors, and how much is attributable to Dixie itself?

When I was growing up, Utah's "Dixie" consisted of several small, tight-knit farming communities strung like beads along a small desert river. Set in the midst of wild red rocks and drifting sand dunes later captured by Hollywood (John Wayne starred in movies filmed in the area when I was growing up), these little towns huddled together against the surrounding wilderness, a group of tiny oases in the midst of the desert.

Even in the 1950s, most Dixie people were descendants of the Mormon pioneer families who first came to the southwestern corner of Utah a century earlier. The call to conquer the red desert sands was issued by their prophet, Brigham Young. Many of the families thus called were originally from the South—the Carolinas, Georgia, and Tennessee. Because their purpose was to raise southern crops, such as cotton, pomegranates, and figs, and to establish an outpost to guard the southern boundary of the Mormon territories, this part of Utah came to be known as "Dixie."

Unlike its counterpart in the southern United States, Utah's Dixie was not a hospitable environment for agriculture. The soil was barren and filled with alkali salts that came to the surface when water was applied. Wood was scarce, and homes were built from native rock or adobe fashioned from the abundant clay. The Virgin River, named by early Spanish explorers, was anything but pure. A capricious source of water, it dried up in the summer heat one week and the next ripped out dams and ditches with flash floods. But by working together, the settlers eventually prevailed, building dams that held and irrigation ditches that watered fields, gardens, orchards, and pastures.

Out of the struggle and the isolation came an extraordinary sense of community. Even in the desert, the pattern of settlement followed the plan for the City of Zion established by Joseph Smith and continued by Brigham Young after the exodus to the West. The City of Zion plat called for communities to be laid out in neat blocks, extending outward from a central common block containing the meetinghouse and other community buildings. It was also requisite that the streets be wide enough for a wagon pulled by a full team of horses to be able to turn around. Beyond the town were the agricultural lands farmed by the community's residents, but most people lived in homes in town, four to a block, each lot with its own garden and perhaps a small orchard, a barn and enclosure for the animals, chicken coops, and other outbuildings.

The settlements of Utah's Dixie followed that pattern, adapted to the harsher realities of the desert. Besides being just about as far south as settlements could be and still be in Utah, the Dixie communities were nearly 2,000 feet lower in elevation than the rest of Utah. This made for mild winters, but extremely hot and dry summers.

As was the case elsewhere in the Mormon West, each of Dixie's miniature cities of Zion was a diverse community of families who looked on their efforts to wrest a living from the land as contributing to the day when Christ would reestablish the heavenly City of Zion on earth. Community life centered around the meetinghouse, which often served as a school during the week, a social center on weekends, and a place of worship on Sundays. Although there were inevitable differences and difficulties between individuals and families, the settlers still considered themselves as spiritual brothers and sisters, children of God, capable of coming together as a community divinely ordained and with millennial purpose.

My own roots go back to some of those families who came to help settle Washington, one of the earliest Dixie communities, in the 1850s and 1860s. They were among those who endured the refining fire of the region's touch-and-go beginnings to see their town survive and eventually prosper.

My great-grandfather George Washington Gill Averett was the watermaster, the individual in charge of the dam, canals, and ditches that supplied the community's lifeblood. For nearly twenty years he oversaw the building—and rebuilding—of a series of diversion dams that would periodically be swept away by flash floods. Another ancestor, Woodruff Alexander, with his young and frail Welsh wife, Martha, endured a harrowing experience with Indian marauders at a remote cattle ranch before being rescued by relatives who had assumed that they were dead and were coming to recover their bodies. My great-great-grandfather William Darby Cooper was a carpenter and cooper (barrel maker). He died of pneumonia after working for hours in waist-deep water making emergency repairs on the water wheel of the pioneer cotton mill. Others were farmers, carpenters, schoolteachers, and homemakers, contributing to the growth and increasing stability of the little southern Utah communities. Descending from those pioneer lines, both my parents were products of the strong culture and spirit of Mormon Dixie.

My personal recollection of my ancestors begins with my

great-grandmother Margaret Alexander Averett, daughter of the couple who survived the Indian raid. My dad adored her. I was only six years old when she died, but I can still remember her gray hair pulled back in a bun, her wrinkled face, her kind smile, her hugging arms, and her soft voice. She was widowed in her early thirties, when my great-grandfather died from a lung disease contracted in the mines of Nevada. After she raised her family of eight, she stayed on in the old family home in Washington.

As a growing grandson, my dad was given the responsibility to care for Great-grandmother Averett. He took this responsibility seriously, staying with her often, making sure the outside chores were performed, and learning to meet her standards. He continued fulfilling these responsibilities even after he was married. The wood had to be chopped and stacked neatly, the garden planted and irrigated throughout the long, hot summers. Survival required frugality and order. Nature taught in its unforgiving way that winter's meals began with the spring's plowing, the summer's tending, and the autumn's yielding. There was usually enough, but never any to waste. Often when I was tromping hay after my dad had methodically aligned a forkful, or when he nodded at me to arrange the wood he was chopping into an orderly pile, he would tell me stories of Great-grandmother Averett. From listening to those stories and watching my father at work, I knew that the lessons she had taught had become a part of him as well.

Grandmother Florence Averett Cooper, my father's mother, was an important part of my own growing-up years. I was already grown and married when she died in 1969, so I have many wonderful memories of her. It was always a treat to go to her house, where she plied us with delicious homemade bread spread with wrinkled yellow cream (skimmed from the top of the milk pans) and sprinkled with sugar.

The grandchildren's guest bedroom was the coziest place in the world. We would climb the narrow stairs into the attic, go around a kind of storage area, and end up in a bedroom where a fire crackled appealingly in a potbellied stove, keeping Grandma's bedroom and the guest bedroom warm. Snuggling down into the flannel sheets and thick blankets was an experience in total security. It was in this room, enjoying the warmth of the stove, that I did my first "homework." While Grandma was darning socks, she gave me a notebook and pencil and asked me to write all the numbers from 1 to 1,000. I remember working my way through the neatly lined pages: 1, 2, 3, 4, 5, 6, 7, ... until the notebook was completely filled. There, too, Grandma triumphed with me as I sounded out my first word from the first-grade reader: C-L-A-S-S!

On the south side of Grandma Cooper's house stood a huge mulberry tree, so thick with leaves and branches that the sun could not penetrate through it. In the summertime, it was like a cave of cool shadow. Hanging from one of its limbs was Grandma's water jug, wrapped in damp burlap to keep it cool, with a long-handled aluminum dipper beside it. When I was older, and came up from the fields after herding cows or hauling hay, the water jug was a first welcome to her home.

Near the river bottom below Washington is a two-bedroom, red sandstone pioneer house known as the Foster farm, long abandoned but still standing, shaded by gigantic cottonwoods. Grandma Cooper and my grandfather, Erastmus Cooper, were hired to manage the farm in 1912. Two years later, their second child and first son, Evan—my father—was born there. After several years of hard work on the farm, my Grandma and Grandpa Cooper were financially able to purchase their own land and home in lower Washington.

The family that later moved in to replace the Coopers as managers of the Foster farm were, by an amazing coincidence, my future maternal grandparents: Orman and Mildred Wilkins. Their oldest daughter, Glenna, caught my father's eye, and in 1938 he married this seventeen-year-old beauty. They began their life together in St. George, five miles west of Washington.

Even though St. George numbered fewer than 3,000 people in

the late 1930s, it was the largest of the Dixie communities, the county seat, and the hub for nearly a dozen smaller towns in the area. St. George had been favored in its early days as Brigham Young's winter home, and it boasted the first Mormon temple to be completed in the West, as well as a magnificent, red-sandstone, white-steepled tabernacle that would have been the envy of any New England town.

In my lifetime St. George has been "discovered" as a recreation and retirement community, and has mushroomed accordingly. But when my parents moved there in 1938, the city was small and still close in spirit and culture to its pioneer beginnings.

I was born into this culture, a fifth-generation Dixie-ite, on a hot June day. I have heard psychologists claim that a child's values are implanted during the first four or five years of life. I lived those crucial years in a small home built on the sandy site of the first pioneer camp at the east edge of St. George. Just as the pioneers had experienced many "firsts" on that spot of land, I encountered many things for the first time there as well.

One memorable "first" was my first wasp sting, which came when I tried to get a drink from an outdoor tap at the same time a wasp was getting one. I learned never to break queue with a wasp in a water line. I learned all about red ants and their possessiveness when I sat on their domain under a big mesquite tree. I got my first shiner from a calf's hoof as it went bucking to its mother. My deep-seated love for horses began there, with pleas to my father to lift me up on Snowball and "hand me the brains, Dad." The childhood diseases—chicken pox, measles, and mumps—all took their turns with me in that St. George home.

The first and probably greatest inspiration of my young life (at least to that point) occurred underneath that home. The cool crawl space below the house provided our collie, Jerry, with a great escape from the desert heat. I loved the dog and could fit into the same space with no trouble, so I often crawled into the coolness to pet Jerry and think deep four-year-old thoughts. I remember the day I contemplated names, and what name I would most like to be called. Suddenly it hit me! I crawled out from under the porch, raced around the house, dashed up the incline to the back stair, and breathlessly hollered to my mother: "Mama! You could call me Tommy Boy Yell!" Surely there couldn't have been a better name—ever.

I laugh now to think what my mother must have thought, but she only smiled and agreed. A short time later, after I had gone back outside to play, I heard her call my new name, "Tommy Boy Yelllll ..." Joyfully, I ran to see what my mom wanted. All my life, when Mom wanted to get my attention, all she had to do was call the magic words: "Tommy Boy Yell!"

After Great-grandmother Averett's death, my father purchased her old pioneer adobe home in south Washington, a sturdy house built in the 1870s and still shaded by ancient ash and mulberry trees. My first memory of our new home began with a headache.

We were in the process of moving from St. George into Great-grandmother's house. It was a warm spring day and I was riding in the back of our 1940 Dodge truck, "holding down" the Maytag washing machine. As we reached the lane that led to our new home and started up the short, steep incline, the washing machine broke loose. Both of us bounced out of the bed of the truck, landed on the hard-packed road, and rolled down the incline. Miraculously, the heavy washing machine bounced over me, but I landed on my head, causing a headache that I remember to this day. I recall my mother jumping out of the truck, gathering me in her arms, and rushing me down the street to Grandma Cooper's house to dry the tears and soothe the pain in a cool bath.

Although my beginnings in this new home were bumpy, it didn't take me long to get acquainted with Washington. The heart of town consisted of four buildings: the meetinghouse, schoolhouse, post office, and general store. The old red-sandstone meetinghouse, built in 1877, was tucked behind the only slightly newer two-story school. The school, a four-room facility with a small gymnasium, was the hub for wedding receptions, community dances, and the school plays that Principal Victor Iverson always had the children put on at Christmas and Easter. Directly across the main street was Abner's General Store, which doubled as the gossip corner where friends met while picking up their groceries and hardware. My first pair of beloved Levi's came from there.

Just behind Abner's store was the post office, located in Widow Stephens's house, where the daily ritual of checking the mail was a big event. Typically, at around 10:30 A.M., Mama would send someone to fetch the mail. Maybe there would be a letter from Granny Wilkins or Great-grandmother Murray.

If you walked five blocks from the center of Washington in any direction, you were out of town. To the south lay the irrigated fields, darkly green in the summer sun beyond the silver ribbon of the now-tamed river. To the east and west, the highway extended away across black, lava-capped ridges to Salt Lake City or Los Angeles and the larger world. To the north, beyond the life-giving springs that made Washington possible, a series of salmon-and-white sandstone cliffs and lava terraces rose toward the sheer wall of Pine Valley Mountain, forming a majestic backdrop ten thousand feet high for our little community.

Although I was only nine, I remember well the process of remodeling that came four years after our move. With the arrival of a new baby sister, we had clearly outgrown Great-grandmother Averett's two-bedroom home. Besides, it had no indoor plumbing. In fact, I learned to roller-skate on the hard-packed path that led to the outhouse.

Dad first built a temporary one-room shelter with a wood-burning stove at one end for cooking and heating and a bed at the other. Ever after, we respectfully called it the "Dog House." Mama, Dad, and baby Kallie stayed there during the year the remodeling project lasted. In the summer months, we three older sisters slept outside on a bed between the pomegranate tree and the rosebush. But during the winter, I slept at Granny Wilkins's house, seven blocks away, while my sisters Margarette and Christine went to Grandma Cooper's, a block down the street, until the job was finished.

All the family's available time was spent on the project, during which we extensively remodeled and modernized the original pioneer structure. We plastered the soft adobe walls, rebuilt the entire roof, added new windows, and constructed a new kitchen and three bedrooms.

This was not an easy feat. Consider that Dad's "help" consisted of Mama and three girls under the age of twelve. Together we carried the cinder block for the new walls of the addition. Together we put up the roof. Together we hauled the red sand from the river bottom for the cement foundation. Dad would hitch up our team of horses to the wagon—a truck would have gotten stuck in the sand. We all brought our shovels, jumped on the flatbed wagon, and drove to the river bottom. Then we shoveled sand onto the wagon bed until Dad pronounced the load big enough but not too heavy for the team to pull. We would climb on top of the sand for the ride back home.

On one particular trip to the river bottom, Christine kept scratching at her knee. My mother, her suspicions aroused by some nameless instinct, pulled up Christine's pant leg to expose a scorpion—common to the desert sands. Dad's big hands quickly brushed it off before it could sting her.

Nearly a year later, we proudly moved into our new home knowing that it really was ours—we had each contributed to the work and we each felt a strong sense of personal ownership. That home would be the setting for many important and lasting childhood memories.

Some of those enduring memories have to do with gunnysacks. This humble bag, made from coarse burlap fabric woven from fibers of jute or hemp, has been a basic storage and shipping container for centuries. A gunnysack has its own unique odor, and I can't pick up one today without its scent bringing back wonderful memories of my childhood years. Gunnysacks were the storage containers for the delicious pine nuts we gathered and roasted in the fall. They held grain for our farm animals and, wrapped around a water jug and moistened, kept our water cool when we worked in the field. We tamped them into the dirt banks of our little diversion dams in the irrigation ditch to keep them stable; we hung wet bags over the screened hutch that sat in the shade of the mulberry trees, turning it into a "refrigerator" for our milk and cheese.

In my parents' generation, many wonderful things came in gunnysacks. Even in his later years, Dad carried a vivid memory of his delightful surprise at finding a single orange in a stocking on Christmas morning. How carefully it was peeled and distributed among all waiting hands, with small fingers wiggling to be noticed first! The orange had come from Uncle Harry, who by horse and wagon had returned home for Christmas from faraway California, bringing in a gunnysack a few precious oranges to disperse carefully among several families.

This story, when Dad told it to his grandchildren, brought expressions of wonderment to their faces. The idea that one gunnysack of oranges lovingly brought by horse and wagon could become the highlight of a family's Christmas celebration seemed incomprehensible to children who passed loaded counters of oranges at the local supermarket every day.

I can see now that in their lives, my mother and father crossed over a long suspension bridge of time, packing over their shoulders a gunnysack brimming with many things. Some of the items in the sack were the old methods, the old ways of accomplishing daily tasks. Struggling along the way, continually meeting the challenges of change, my parents traded those old ways for new conveniences.

But as they discarded and replaced many of the methods and tools they had originally carried in it, Mama and Dad still clung to the old burlap gunnysack. It was the real treasure: the values and traditions of grandparents and great-grandparents to be passed along to the next generation.

In the years since the gunnysack passed to my generation, I too have found that many of my childhood ways of doing things no longer work in the culture that has evolved. The methods and the means may have changed, but the real treasure of my family's values and traditions stays the same. And my children and their children need them even more now than I did when I learned them under the tutelage of Mama and Dad.

So I keep the burlap gunnysack, a reminder that my generation too must pass its treasured values and traditions to those who come after.

Acorn

I came from Utah's Dixie and now, after moving all over the globe and making homes in many other places, here I am, back in Dixie. How can a place and a culture have such a hold on a person? As strange as it appears to some, my attraction to my roots does not seem unusual to those born and raised with the red sand of Dixie between their toes. Coming home to this special place elicits a feeling that can't be compared to anything else. A friend describes the inborn Dixie spirit: "It's just something in my soul that longs and lingers."

I see in the current hunger for community a sense of the connectedness that I felt growing up in Washington, Utah, a place of kith, kin, and kindness, where a whole community felt invested in its children. I know that such communities can be rebuilt with intelligent investing of time, talent, and love.

Notice that money is not on the list. As important as it may be, money is useful only for such things as contracts and commodities. Communities are about caring. During my childhood, we never had more than a marginal economic existence, but the home created by Evan and Glenna Cooper was a solid foundation for our lives, a place where love was expressed and happy memories were born. Without necessarily understanding what they were doing, my parents—through their example and the things they expected from us—passed on the core values of our family and our community.

The Lessons of Wash Day

Because of the lack of modern conveniences in our small rural community, simple daily tasks often took a long time, sometimes even full days, to complete. Since laundry was done only once a week, "wash day" was exactly that—a whole day. After chores and breakfast, we would sort out seven or eight batches of clothes on the kitchen floor to begin the process. At the time, we felt blessed to have the latest technology in washers: the Double Dexter Washing Machine. It provided the convenience of an electric, double-tub wringer, right on our very own porch. Instead of having to slave over a washboard and tub, we had a Double Dexter.

After Mama had heated a large pail of water on the stove and dumped it into the washer, she filled the remainder of the washtub and the entire rinse tub with cold water from the outside garden hose. She always tied two or three bluing balls in an old rag to float around in the rinse water and dissolve while she filled the tub. I never did quite understand how the bluing somehow acted as a whitener, but it kept Mama's whites looking clean and new, despite the yellowing characteristics of the homemade lye soap we used. White clothes would always go into the washer's first batch, then towels and dish towels, colored items, and finally Levi's, overalls, and Dad's greasy cooking clothes.

Though Mama used the same water for several batches, just filling the tubs and draining the water out onto the lawn once or twice was time-consuming—not to mention the tedious process of putting each individual article through the wringer to squeeze out the sudsy water before the item dropped into the rinse tub. The wringer came into play again as the clothes passed from the rinse tub to the laundry basket. Mama then artfully hung the clothes on the line with clothespins while waiting for the next two loads to cycle through the washer.

I recognize now that each wash day an unstated homemakers' washline competition went on in my hometown. This was no doubt one of the reasons that Mama took great pride in how her clothes were hung on the line. Her fun-loving, even artistic, side came out in how she hung up our laundry. All the full skirts hung upside down by the hem in a row. All the blouses were lined up, also upside down, to billow in the drying desert wind, the clothespins staking down the seams that ran from sleeve to hem. The towels took two lines and were hung square, corner to corner. The finished product was almost like a visual representation of a full-blown orchestra, with distinct sections for brass, woodwinds, and strings, all performing harmoniously.

When we children were small, our task was to fill and drain the tubs and to hang the socks over the barbed-wire fence, each sock between two barbs. As we grew tall enough to reach the clothesline, we were promoted to hanging the towels and dish towels. However, Mama always insisted on meticulously hanging the colorful blouses, skirts, and dresses herself. Her artistic, joy-filled attention to that weekly labor was a great lesson in the satisfaction to be had from work done well.

The Electrolux

Recently, Hyrum and I visited an oriental shop so that Hyrum could buy his year's stash of li hing mui, a sour-salty dried plum. As I waited for him to make his purchase, I scanned the contents of the many square glass containers. One, filled with pine nuts, brought a rush of memories of gathering pine nuts from the scrubby pinyon pines of my home country.

Oddly enough, connected with those nuts was a love story—my parents'. Those pine nuts had a lot to do with romance, consistent work, shared goals, and caregiving. In the friendly, effective, and above all loyal relationship of my parents, I didn't see many flickers of dime-novel or Errol-Flynn-type romance. But I saw something better. It was an Electrolux vacuum cleaner. And, fittingly enough, it began with the exhausting labor of harvesting pine nuts.

Almost every October, my parents packed up the family, our

camping gear, and some tarps and turpentine, and we would head
for the mountains of Panaca, Nevada, a hundred miles away. We
always took Uncle Frank Prince, the last of the Dixie old-timers, and
he invariably made the trip lively.

Usually we left after school on a Friday and traveled to the
upland hills where the pine trees were thick and heavily loaded
with pine cones. We set up camp by clearing the fallen cones away
to make room for our bedrolls on the soft blanket of pine needles.
Uncle Frank cooked a Dutch-oven dinner of biscuits and beans.
Then, to the smell of the smoke from the campfire, we snuggled
down in the thick bedrolls that kept us warm in the chilly fall air.
High in the black night sky, brilliant stars cast their spell; eyelids
closed and dreams began.

I remember waking up to the sun kissing my face. From my
cozy bedroll, I watched Dad rekindle the fire and Mama place thick
pieces of bacon in the frying pan. Moments later, the smell of siz-
zling bacon caused growling hunger pains, inspiring my sisters and
me to leave our warm beds for the crisp morning air to devour our
breakfast of biscuits, bacon, fried eggs, and hot chocolate.

Even before breakfast, Uncle Frank had scouted out the best
trees and placed the tarps in position for the day's work. We all put
on our gloves and old work clothes. Using rakes or long sticks, Dad
and Uncle Frank shook the pine branches to knock the pine cones
onto the tarp. My job was to assist in this effort by shinnying up
the tree to shake the higher branches. In that initial fall, many pine
nuts would be jarred free from the cones.

After we had gathered a large pile of cones on the tarp, everyone would surround the canvas and lift an edge, causing the cones
to roll to the center. Then we poured the pine cones out into a cus-
tom-built wooden box with a wire screen bottom. The holes in the
screen were large enough to allow the pine nuts but not the cones
to drop through to a tarp below. Two people, one on each end,
picked up the box and shook it, bouncing the pine cones one more
time to loosen the last remaining seeds. We emptied the pine cones

from the box and picked up the tarp again to funnel the nuts into the waiting burlap gunnysacks. Then we moved to another tree and started the process again.

By the end of the day, we had pine gum all over our hands and gloves, faces and clothes. Dirt and dust stuck to the gum, leaving sticky streaks and spots everywhere. But it did no good to clean up until the gummy job was done. When we had a couple of hundred pounds of nuts in our gunnysacks, we loaded them in the truck. Then, and only then, we shed our gloves and sticky clothes and began the arduous task of rubbing the pine gum off our hands and faces with turpentine-soaked rags. Weary but happy, we packed up our camp and headed for home. I was happy because I knew that the next time I saw those pine nuts, I would be sitting on the sandstone hearth near the blazing fire with a bowl of freshly roasted nuts on my lap. I would crack the shells with my front teeth, throw the shells into the flames, and toss the nutmeats into my mouth. Nothing could be more sumptuous and succulent.

On one such occasion, in early December, my sensuous feast was disturbed by a knock on the door. Mama answered, and before she could inquire about the nature of the visitor's business, a stranger briskly stepped inside, hefting a large cardboard box with a handle. This boldness caused my father to rise up out of his chair and demand, "What do we have here?"

The stranger proudly announced, "I'm a vacuum cleaner salesman and I understand you have need for a vacuum. I have in this box a vacuum that will take care of all your cleaning needs."

We all exchanged curious glances as the salesman opened his box and lifted out an elongated, rounded canister on wheels, which he set on the floor. He reached in again, pulled out a long, thickly woven cloth hose, and poked it in a hole in the end of the canister, which bore the letters E-L-E-C-T-R-O-L-U-X.

He turned to his box again to remove two shiny silver tubes. He locked the two together into one long tube and then attached it to the end of the hose. Again reaching in the box, he took out four different-shaped metallic gadgets, explaining, "Now, this is your upholstery attachment. It will clean your couches, chairs, and draperies. This round one with soft bristles will dust walls, furniture, windows, lamp shades, and bookshelves—virtually anything that collects dust. You can throw away your oily dust rag. This needle-shaped attachment gets in all those hard-to-reach places: behind your fridge, under the stove, in corners. It can even suck dead flies out of windowsills." (I was particularly impressed with that feature.) "And last, but certainly not least, is this floor attachment, which can handle virtually any mess." With that, he pulled out a small sack and dumped dirt on our floor.

Mama gasped in disbelief.

"Oh, don't worry, ma'am," the salesman continued. "This Electrolux will have your floor clean as a whistle in no time." With that he unwound the electric cord and, with a nod to Margarette, said, "Hey, little girl, will you plug this into the electrical outlet?"

Excitedly, she did so. In seconds the unfamiliar whirring began, and the man began going over the asphalt-tiled front-room floor in neat swaths, just as my dad did with his tractor in the hay field. Sure enough, that vacuum did what the salesman said it would do. Then he launched into his final pitch: "Now, wouldn't this make a great addition to your house? Why, you could have this place slicked up in no time. This is my last model; seeing as it's a demonstration vacuum, I'll give it to you tonight for twenty dollars off."

"Mama, can we?" all three of us girls begged in unison.

I looked at my mother for her reaction. I really wanted it, and I could tell by the way she looked at Dad that she did too, but she discreetly shook her head no. To the salesman she politely said, "We really can't afford it at this time of year, as badly as we would all like it."

My dad agreed, "Yeah, you better box it up and take it away. I'll help you on out." Dad walked outside with the deflated salesman.

The next morning, after Mama had gone to work, I was

surprised to see the salesman coming up the walk. Dad invited him in and asked him to wait. The next thing I knew, Dad came in with a gunnysack three-quarters full of our precious pine nuts. I overheard the salesman say, "Well, sir, here's your receipt, 'One Deluxe Electrolux; Paid in Pine Nuts (100 lbs.).'"

I don't know where Dad hid the box. All I know is that it showed up under the tree on Christmas morning, beautifully wrapped and bearing a tag, "To Glenna." Attached to the top with a red ribbon was a single pine cone.

Mama and the Sparklers

My parents passed through life with a quick eye for the comical, greeting the ludicrous with gales of laughter in which there was no sting of mockery. The gifts of laughter and a keen sense of humor were sparks that drew them together, lighting many a weary hour.

For my dad, steadily and steadfastly turning his hand to each new job as it came up and doing his uncomplaining best, duty comprised very nearly all there was to life. Mama and Dad farmed. They worked in a local restaurant, Dad cooking while Mama waited tables. They ran a rest home for years, providing cleanliness, care, and good cheer to people slipping toward death. Every day was hard work, and they never complained. Mama settled to the same rhythm as Dad, pulling cheerfully in double harness and leaving no chore undone, yet she bubbled with gaiety and fun, purely enjoying the seasons and the sunsets. Glenna Fern Wilkins grew up as one of six children in a hard-working farming family and was only seventeen years old when she married. Even with the rigors she knew most of her life, she always maintained a youthful, fun-loving, adventurous spirit. In the cracks between the required chores, she could always find fun.

It was the third of July. In the late afternoon, when Mama pulled up in the black Dodge truck and got out carrying a grocery bag, I paid attention. Normally I wouldn't have noticed the contents of the brown paper sack (usually basic commodities such as flour, sugar, and eggs), but as she approached, something different—maybe frivolous—poking out of the top caught my eye. I followed the bag to the kitchen table. I was right. Nothing could have prevented me from carefully taking out one of the long, narrow boxes to scrutinize every detail. It was a bright red box with patterns of white starbursts and streaming tails. The full cellophane window on the front exposed the thin, gray sparklers that always reminded me of the cattails in the marshes on the river bottom.

My mother, noticing my keen interest, reminded me that the next day was the Fourth of July. "Gail," she said, "tomorrow night I'm going to put on the grandest sparkler show you've ever seen."

Mama's words sent shivers of excitement through my nine-year-old body. I couldn't wait for it to get dark, so I could go out to my summer bed between the pomegranate tree and the rosebush. The anticipation made it difficult for me to fall asleep, but I must have, because the next thing I knew I was aroused by the traditional cannon shots and musical strains of "The Stars and Stripes Forever." The Granny Band (one granny being my own, who played the harmonica) woke up the town every Fourth of July by parading up and down the streets rendering rousing, patriotic music. Quentin Nisson (who was lovingly called "Abner" and ran the General Store) would set up his old upright piano on a flatbed truck and arrange folding chairs for the band members, who donned long dresses, bonnets, and other pioneer garb for the event. About once every block they would fire the cannon, which trailed behind the truck.

This day, Mama didn't have to work very hard to hustle us through our chores and housecleaning duties; we knew that as soon as we were finished we could go over to the park for the annual Fourth of July games and races. There were foot races, three-legged races, wheelbarrow races, egg tosses, balloon tosses, and needle-threading contests for the men. Each contest was divided into various age or gender categories, so everyone had a chance to win a prize. There was also plenty of lemonade and watermelon for all.

The full day's activities ended with the setting of the sun. As dark set upon us, our family (except Dad, who had gone to work) anxiously raced home to prepare for Mama's promised sparkler show. Mama, with flashlight in hand, let me and my sisters bring out the sparkler boxes and stack them on the top step of the cement stairs leading to the road. She followed us with the box of matches. "Now," she said, "all of you sit here on the steps." We did, and she began the sparkler show.

She lit one sparkler, then another, and then another. Sometimes she handed us each a sparkler and let us hold it to wave back and forth in the air. Sometimes she connected two sparklers together by bending the ends into hooks, then lit both ends and sent the two gyrating high into the air. They flew upward, lighting up the sky, then spiraled down and landed in the road to burn themselves out. One time, in her excitement and effort to give us a really good show, she threw a half dozen sparklers, all hooked together, a little farther than she had anticipated. They landed across the street in our neighbor's wheat field.

Immediately the field lit up with flames. Panicking, Mama hollered for us to get the garden hose. We grabbed it, turned the tap on, and raced across the street, spraying water on all the tiny fire patches. At about the same time, our neighbor saw what was happening and quickly grabbed his hose as well. Any empty hands filled buckets of water from the ditch that ran by or soaked gunnysacks to throw on the scattered flames. It was plenty exciting for a few minutes, but it didn't stop Mama's sparkler show the next year—or for years to come.

Mama had creative ways of expressing her wonderful sense of humor. Halloween was one outlet for such expression. Each Halloween, with great secrecy, she would plan and plot with us over how we would disguise ourselves to go about the town trick-or-treating.

It was a small town, so it was not difficult or time-consuming to cover the entire community, knocking on every door with a "Trick-or-Treat!" Some of the people would make us do a trick, such as reciting a poem or singing a song, to earn our treat.

The year I was ten, I went trick-or-treating with Uncle Kendyl, who, despite his exalted title, was my own age and also my good friend. We dressed up as farmers and managed to come up with the money to buy simple masks at Abner's Store. That night, since we were in the middle of remodeling Great-grandmother Averett's house, I was to stay at my Granny Wilkins's house with Kendyl.

We returned after an hour of trick-or-treating, our bags bulging with treats, which we dumped out on the living-room floor. We were busy comparing candy, swapping items, and critiquing the contributions of the donors when we heard a knock on the door. I ran to get it as quickly as I could, knowing that it was probably more trick-or-treaters.

I was right, but the visitors weren't children. There in the doorway stood two huge ghosts. Aunt Nola Wilkins invited them in. As I stepped quickly aside, the two big ghosts floated in and sat down together on the piano bench, just in front of our piles of candy. I immediately went back to guard my candy and look up at those enormous ghosts. They had to be adults. Granny came in from the kitchen, wiping her wet hands on her apron.

"Who are you?" asked Aunt Nola.

The ghosts gave no answer.

"Do you live in this town?"

They nodded.

"Do we know you?"

Again a nod.

"Do you live close by?"

The ghosts shrugged.

Kendyl and I, intrigued, joined in the questioning, but the

ghosts' identity remained a mystery. Then the ghost nearest me looked down and, behind the hole cut for its mouth, grimaced at me. I could see the teeth and part of the lips. My mind began to race. I had seen that grimace and those teeth before. But where? I searched my memory. Where, where?

Suddenly it came to me. I burst out, "I know you! I've seen those teeth before." The ghost chuckled and then I was absolutely sure. It was my mother. The other ghost was my Aunt Nola Cooper.

I think often of what it meant that my mother was willing to ruin two perfectly good sheets to step out of her workaday identity as Glenna Cooper for a few hours to mystify and delight us children. I hope I show the same imagination with my own children.

The Swimming Hole

One of the lasting lessons of my childhood was that fun was paid for with work. Dad's tone of voice was serious when he reminded us, "Work before play." But Mama, more adventurous and light-hearted, taught us, "Work pays for fun." She contrived and schemed so that we had fun while working and our work had a pay-off of fun.

It was July in Dixie. This particular week seemed to have passed slowly, but at last it was Saturday morning. I was excited because Mama had promised my sisters and me—and any friends we wanted to have along—that if we would get the Saturday's work done (chores, housework, cleaning the yard, and mowing the lawn), she would take us swimming in the old swimming hole. There could not be a greater reward on a hot summer day.

I rose early, eager to get my work done. I called my friends down the street to see if they would come help with the chores so they could enjoy the swimming adventure as well. Being really good at delegating, I quickly assigned my sisters and two or three of my neighborhood friends to do this and that chore. David would mow the lawn, Christine would clean the kitchen, Margarette would vacuum the house, Kathy would clean the bathroom, and I would dust the furniture and sweep and mop the floors. Each sister had to clean her own room. Periodically Mama would call for our help, and we would hurry outside to hang a batch of laundry.

After a morning of hard work, we all reunited in the living room, excited to report that at last our jobs were done. Mama easily talked us into some baloney or egg sandwiches for lunch, with cool milk to wash them down, as final preparation for our long, hot trip to the swimming hole. Finally she gave us the go-ahead: "Let's run and get our swimming suits on." And away we all went, hiking the mile and a half to our destination.

This hike, in retrospect, was a journey in itself, but nearing the swimming hole brought one last challenge—the climb up the steep, rocky Warm Springs Hill. After struggling to the top, we could look down and actually see the water hole, nestled among green trees and reeds, a hundred yards away. That glistening pool was an oasis in the red sands.

As with any swimming hole, the likelihood of catching some boys "skinny dipping" was pretty high; thus, over time, some unwritten courtesies had evolved. This day was no different. Seeing boys in the water, we signaled, "Yoohoo! Girls coming!" then turned our backs and rested a moment while the boys scrambled into the bushes for their clothes. We then raced down the hill, flinging off our shirts, and jumped into the cool, clear water. It was a well-earned reward.

My mother jumped right in the pool with us and led us in the water games that we all loved to play: Blind Man's Bluff, Marco Polo, and Water Tag. When she felt that our bodies needed it, she made us get out to rest for a few minutes on the grassy banks in the warm sunshine. By the time our suits were dry, we were pleading with Mama to let us get back in, and we started the swimming and splashing all over again. Too soon, Mama ordered us out of the pool to dry off one last time and begin our downhill trek home.

Thinking back on that glorious Saturday afternoon and many others like it, I can't help getting a lump in my throat as I now realize the time commitment, physical effort, and loving protection my mother quietly offered. Gently, effectively, she taught us the value of work before play, cooperation, fun, and friendship.

I don't know what it meant to my mother to spend the whole afternoon going for a swim. I don't know if she savored and honored her instinct for play. But I do know that it meant something important to me that my mother would play with us.

Yes, she fed, clothed, and bossed her children around, just like other mothers. There was never any mention of the "rules" she broke to enter into our world of play and imagination. But those crossings-over showed that she was literally on our side. She was no censorious judge of our play, nor did she seem to be consciously indulging childishness in a way that communicated her expectation that we would someday abandon it. Her heart was with us in sympathy. I felt her liking and her love through that play in a way that I could not articulate until years later.

The adult world was my father's world—he always said that he never had a childhood. As the eldest boy in his family, he was put to work as soon as he was physically able. Dad was creative and artistic, and a natural musician—probably an inherited gift from his great-grandfather William Darby Cooper, who handcrafted his own violin and dulcimer and was a renowned musician in the Dixie region. He loved to tease, but, of necessity, order and productivity governed his life. My mother usually stood squarely in that world beside him. But in moments like those July afternoons, without ever saying it, she taught us clearly with her actions, "You've earned fun. You've paid for it with your work. And so have I." She modeled the difference between being a hard worker and being a workaholic. For Glenna Cooper, there was work, but there was also glorious fun.

As a result, I always thought of my own future children as people I wanted to be with, work with, play with, and enjoy.

The Magic of the Mulberry Tree

Another important lesson of my childhood came not from the example or influence or teaching of my parents, but from self-discovery. This experience seemed to mark an important turning point, one of those times when a person's worldview changes.

One of my favorite childhood play areas was in back of my house, between two large (to my eyes, mammoth) mulberry trees standing about ten feet apart. Along the base of those two giant trees ran a wide, shallow, sandy-bottomed ditch that continued past the trees and on down into the garden below. The purpose of the ditch became apparent every Friday at exactly 1:15 P.M., when irrigation water came down it into the garden.

My sister, my friends, and I would play in the sandy-bottomed ditch and at the base of the north mulberry tree, pretending that we were farmers or ranchers. That game kept us occupied for hours on any day except on Fridays at 1:15, when the water came down the ditch; or on Saturdays, because the area was too muddy; or on Sundays, because we were expected to observe the Sabbath day.

By Monday our farm or ranch land, whichever we decided it would be that day, was dry and ready for play again. We lived in pretend houses on top of the ditch bank between the big roots of the north mulberry tree. We built roads down the ditch bank, then drove our toy trucks and tractors or rode our little horses from our houses down the steep grade to the sandy bottom of the ditch.

Then we began the project of building our corrals and fencing our lands. In order to do this, we built roads into the "forest" of nearby shrubs. There we gathered twigs and cut or broke them into four-inch fence posts. We hauled our fence posts in our trucks out of the forest and back to our sandy farmland, where we poked them into the ground about two inches apart and strung kite string between them to make the fence. We always made two string-wire fences; we wanted to make sure that the cows and horses would not go astray.

We spent many enjoyable hours building fancy ranches and farms down in the ditch. Our hands, faces, clothes, seams, creases, and pockets were always caked with red sand by the time we finished playing. Occasionally we suffered a bite from one of the many big red ants that seemed to think this was *their* play area. However, our biggest tragedy occurred every Friday at 1:15 P.M., when our farms and ranches would be flooded, our fences and fence posts washed downstream. Often we forgot to take in our animals, trucks, trailers, and tractors before the Friday flood hit, and we would have to retrieve them from the garden below on the following Monday.

One Monday when I was about eleven, I was sitting on the ditch surveying the damage to my farm. I realized that the project of rebuilding, which used to be play for me, now seemed like a lot of work. As I flicked a big red ant off my shoe, it occurred to me, "Gail, playing in a ditch is dirty play. What's more, you're not accomplishing anything; no matter how big and nice and neat you build your farms and roads, you are building on a sandy foundation. When the Friday flood comes, all is lost. You can't enjoy your good work or continue to build on it." I then thought, "Instead of looking down into the ditch and building all those neat corrals, fences, roads, and houses on such a sandy foundation, why don't you look up and find something worthwhile to invest your efforts in?"

As my eyes followed my train of thought, the first thing I noticed was the mammoth mulberry tree to the south. As I stood up in the ditch, I wondered what the world would look like from the top of a mulberry tree. My quest became to find out.

My first challenge was figuring out how to get up in the tree. The trunk of this huge mulberry was as big around as a semitrailer tire and extended as high as a basketball standard before any of its branches began to spread out. It was impossible to wrap my legs around the tree to climb, nor were there any branches low enough for me to grasp to pull myself up.

I first attempted to throw my father's lasso rope over the lowest branch and hoist myself up, but my efforts were thwarted by the thick leaves and branches. My second plan required a lot of work and some trial and error. Obtaining my father's permission to use some old lumber he had stacked in a bin, I sawed some boards into two-foot lengths. I then rounded up some big nails and a hammer and proceeded to make my stair ladder up the trunk. I attached the first two boards easily by hammering a big nail through the center of each into the trunk. I should have known it was too easy, for when I put my weight on the stair, the board turned on the nail and I was again standing on the ground. I learned that I must nail both ends of the board to the tree.

My next attempts (and errors) came with my trying to engineer height so I could hammer in the nails to hold the last two stairs in place. Unhelped by a chair, then by a box on top of the chair, then another box on top of the first box, I finally scrapped that plan after some very anxious and unstable moments.

My last effort—and success—came with the toil of dragging an old, unused rabbit pen from the corral up to the tree. This was approximately the distance of a baseball diamond from home plate all the way around the bases. It was a long haul, but when I reached my destination, the height and stability of the rabbit pen enabled me to finish the ladder, each step nailed securely to the trunk of the tree.

My finished ladder endured the final test when I climbed the five stairs, grasped a branch, and swung myself into the main fork in the huge branches of the mulberry tree. What an exhilarating feeling of joy filled my soul! My heart beat like the wings of a dragonfly; excitement erased the aching muscles and the dripping sweat. I had achieved my quest.

Standing in the fork of that giant mulberry tree, I could see forever. To the south lay the lazily winding Virgin River, glistening in the sun. Below the river I could see rectangular fields, each wearing a proud, unique shade of green. Above me was only vast blueness, broken by occasional wisps of white cotton. To the east was the red-orange, mountainous strength of Zion National Park, the highest peaks capped with snowy whiteness. The north view took in the massive bulk of Pine Valley Mountain with the red hills of Dixie snuggled against its base.

From my height in the mulberry tree, a new world with endless horizons opened before me. The excitement was still building in my heart when, at that moment, I looked down. The ditch below, in which I had been sitting all morning, was cold, dark, and gloomy. The red ants were trailing in, out, and over the roots of the north mulberry tree and down into the ditch.

I shuddered as I realized all the wonderful things I had been missing by playing in the ditch at the roots of the tree. My view was blocked by my very position. My dreams were washed down the stream every Friday at 1:15 P.M. After viewing all that I had seen from this magnificent mulberry tree, I would never again be satisfied with the play or the view from the ditch.

Quickly, I refocused my eyes and my thoughts back to my tree. To my pleasant surprise, and seemingly as a bonus for all my hard efforts, I discovered a natural tree house within the tree's limbs and branches. The big limbs had grown out and up like the ribs of a giant, upside-down umbrella, and branches had filled in the spaces between, forming natural walls.

Ideas coursed through my brain as to how I would make one terrific tree house. I immediately obtained equipment and tools and began delegating tasks to my friends and sisters.

By Friday, the terrific tree house was completed. The floor was carpeted, the walls were paneled, and two curtains (contributed and hung by my mother, who for some reason was very excited about this tree house) adorned the natural windows. We were having the time of our lives. We soon discovered that our play was not limited to building temporary roads and fences. Instead we built permanent corrals to house our animals, or, if we were in the mood, we made houses for our dolls. We even consumed our peanut butter sandwiches, cookies, and milk within the walls of our terrific tree house—thanks to Mama's delivery service.

One day, as I was enjoying the last cookie, listening to the birds singing from higher in the tree, and relishing the warmth of sunshine on my back, I heard the familiar sound of rushing water. At first, fear seized my body as I realized it was the 1:15 P.M. Friday flood. I was trying to remember if I had removed all the animals, tractors, and trucks from the ditch.

Then I remembered, and my fears were washed away. Now my hopes, my dreams, my animals, my trucks, and my house were centered on a strong foundation. When the winds, rains, and floods came, this terrific tree house would stand firm. From my mulberry-tree height, I looked down and watched the Friday flood wash my past into the garden.

3

A leaf, a stem, and a brief root shooting down

Values—many of them old-fashioned, all of them desperately needed and clearly teachable—were among the most important things Hyrum and I learned when we were children. My own childhood forged indelible lessons in honesty, prayer, and many other vital principles that I have since tried to share with my children.

Honesty and the Candy Bars

"Gail," called my dad, "take a dozen eggs to Abner's and trade them for a pound of oleomargarine, please."

I had run this three-block errand before, proving myself a dependable seven-year-old capable of being suitably careful with the fragile cargo. Mama packed the eggs in a paper bag and sent me on my way.

I walked through the big store door and put the sack on the counter. Abner carefully opened it and glanced at the contents. "Put 'em in the egg basket, Gail," he said. "And pick up the oleo." When I returned to the counter, he handed me fifteen cents. "There's the change," he said.

I closed my hand around the dime and nickel. Then my eyes fell on a row of Baby Ruth candy bars. It was late in the afternoon, but still two hours before supper. I was ravenous, and we were always starved for sweets. Chewy carmeled nuts. Creamy milk chocolate. I put a dime on the counter and heard myself saying, "Two Baby Ruth candy bars, please."

Pocketing my dad's remaining nickel, I stepped off the porch, peeling back the wrapper on the first bar. Every bite was heavenly. I savored each morsel slowly, then opened the second. It was gone before I turned the corner to our house. I shoved the wrappers out of sight under some bushes.

Suddenly I wondered—would my dad know about the change? I bounced up the front steps, waving the oleo. My mother took it and disappeared into the kitchen. I went back outside to resume my play, but Dad materialized from nowhere. "Gail, where's my change?"

I quickly pulled the nickel out of my pocket and handed it to him.

"Where's the rest?" he asked.

My heart began to race. My palms got sweaty, but I said calmly, "There wasn't any more."

Dad placed his big hand on my shoulder, walked me through the front gate, and steered me down the path to the running board of our old Dodge truck. He sat beside me, his arm around my shoulders.

"You can fight and quarrel, Gail," he said. "You can swear, you can smoke, you can drink, and you can still be a good person. But if you're dishonest, you stop being good. You can't tell the truth sometimes and lie sometimes. Nothing is more important than your integrity, Gail. If you lie to me about a dime, you'll end up lying about more important things."

Tears were running down my cheeks. "I'm sorry, Dad!" I wailed. I knew that what he was saying was true. I had never felt so ashamed, so awful. I clung to his dark blue denim work shirt and sobbed, "I'll never do it again."

His arm closed around me fiercely. I felt his cheek on the top of my head for a moment. Silence was relief—I had learned my lesson, and my dad knew it.

Evan Erastmus Cooper was an honorable man. I never doubted it, even before I knew what honor was. My people had never had a great deal of money. The red soil of the Washington farm yielded its onions, radishes, sugar beets, and alfalfa only reluctantly. Mama worked as a waitress at Dick's Cafe when the family coffers were low. But truth counted for something among the Coopers and the Wilkinses.

Prayer and the Softball

It was summertime. I must have been about seven years old. After the beds were made, the dishes done, and the house straightened up, I would ask my mother the familiar question, "May I go play at Richard's house?" Given her permission, I took the shortcut through the sage and began the one-mile hike from my house to his.

Our favorite game was Bat and Roll. Richard would bat the ball out to me, then lay the bat on the ground pointing in my direction. My job was to field the ball, then roll it back to try to hit the bat. If the ball touched the bat, I became the batter and Richard would go to the field.

One morning when I appeared at his house to continue our game, we could not find the softball. We looked everywhere: behind bushes, under shrubs, around trees, and in tall grass and ditches. The ball was nowhere to be found. I asked Richard to think back and retrace his steps from the last time he had played with the ball. This led us into his house, where we looked under tables, in closets, under chairs and couches. All to no avail.

Finally, he wondered if his mother had put it in the toy box in his bedroom. We dug through the box, looked on his shelves, under the pillows, under the bed—anywhere we thought the softball might be. We were both disappointed that we would be unable to play.

As we stood there, downhearted, suddenly a lesson taught by our teacher in Primary clicked in my mind. I reminded Richard that the teacher had said if ever we were lost, or couldn't find something important, or needed anything, all we needed to do was pray to our Heavenly Father, and he would help us.

Richard replied, "That's right! I remember that."

Without hesitation we knelt at his bedside and simply said, "Heavenly Father, Sister Hall told us that if we ever needed your help, we could kneel down and ask you for it. We want to play softball today and we can't find our ball. Would you help us find it?"

While I still had my head bowed and eyes closed, a vivid picture of where the softball lay came into my mind. Confidently, I leaned down, pulled up the corner of the bedspread, and picked up the ball.

"Okay, Richard," I said matter-of-factly. "Heavenly Father answered our prayer. Let's go play."

From that moment, I knew that God indeed answers prayers. It was the first of several experiences that taught me the reality of that truth. Another such moment came a few years later, when I was a teenager and old enough to drive. My need was much greater than the simple desire to find a softball, but my earlier experience with God helped me to exercise childlike faith in finding something far more precious that was lost.

At the time, I was working as a waitress at the Liberty Cafe in St. George to earn money to attend college. I had dropped my adored dog, Mopsy, off at the veterinarian's office on my way to work. He had recommended she be spayed to minimize the effects of a calcium deficiency she suffered. Because of the bond of loyalty between me and Mopsy, it was hard for me on that Friday morning to leave her at the vet's for the procedure. I knew she would hate it, and I would miss her, too.

Some three hours into my shift, I received a phone call from the vet. Mopsy had escaped. "We cannot find her," he said. "We have looked everywhere, up and down the road, and we just cannot find her."

Frustrated that I couldn't leave work, I anxiously waited for my shift to end at 2:00 P.M., then hurriedly drove to the veterinarian's. Although he was apologetic and tried to explain how the dog had gotten out, all I cared about was that somewhere out there in those vast fields of alfalfa was my little dog, alone, in foreign surroundings, five miles away from home. Some dogs have incredible homing instincts, but Mopsy was a sheltered house dog, with little outdoor experience.

I began my search. I drove up and down the road, hunted through the alfalfa fields near the vet's office, and walked down to the river bottom, whistling and shouting her name. I tried to think like Mopsy. Which way would she go? What route would she take? I looked for her all afternoon, pursuing every possible avenue she might have tried, but to no avail. Finally darkness forced me in.

The next day after work, again I searched and searched. I was frantic, thinking of all the things that could have happened. She had no food or water. What about predators? Could someone have taken her? I extended the radius of my quest past the alfalfa fields, up on the Black Ridge west of St. George, through the city streets, back down to the river. I asked everyone I met if they had seen my dog. Again, no success.

On Sunday, I decided I would fast and pray about finding Mopsy. After church, a strong impression came to me about where to look for her. Improbable as it seemed, I knew I was going to find my dog. I asked my mother if she would drive while I looked. To her disbelief, we drove away from Mopsy's most probable route home toward the other side of Black Ridge, ten miles away. My mom followed my instructions, but the expression on her face told me what she was thinking.

Another impression came: turn left and go toward the Santa Clara fields. As we drove along a dirt road, we stopped often to get out and call for Mopsy. We searched for a long time. My hopes gradually dimmed as we continued driving through the green alfalfa fields, eventually circling back toward St. George. Finally I had to admit defeat. I looked over toward my mother and opened my mouth to say, "Let's go home." Then, through her open car window, I noticed a wave of movement in the alfalfa field beyond the road.

It could have been anything, but I knew.

"Mama, stop the car!" I yelled. I jumped out and ran to the barbed-wire fence, calling "Mopsy? Mopsy?" Just above the top of the alfalfa, her little head popped up in recognition. She bounded toward me as fast as she could, while I crawled through the fence to run and meet her.

I picked her up and hugged her. She simultaneously yapped, licked me, and wriggled hysterically. My mother, tears in her eyes, shook her head in disbelief. Joyfully yet solemnly we drove home, pulling burrs and foxtails out of Mopsy's matted fur. Once again, I had learned that God does hear and answers prayers with a generosity that does not scorn some requests as insignificant. His eye is on the sparrow—and the softball, and a little lost dog.

Working toward a Goal: The Softball Glove

I was taught early that faith and works go hand in hand. In my family we learned faith, we learned work, and we learned faith *in* work. My softball glove was a wonderful test of my faith in work.

I was not very old before I discovered that my gifts lay in the athletic realm. For a female growing up in Dixie in the fifties, the only organized outlet for athletic expression was the Church-sponsored Young Women's softball program. When I graduated from Primary at age twelve and was eligible to play on that team, I could hardly wait until the season began. I was so excited—until I dug out my old softball glove. The horsehair padding was coming out of the worn holes in the leather; the leather thongs that had once held the fingers together were missing. It was flat worn-out. It seemed okay in the sandy backyards and behind the schoolhouse, but now that I was in the big leagues, I had to have a new glove.

I knew it would be futile to go to Mama and Dad with this request. *I* knew I needed a new glove, but I didn't think *they* would feel that I did. Besides, the family finances would never stretch far enough to afford one. So I formulated a plan to obtain a new glove myself—and to have it by the time softball season began.

In the farming community of Washington, early spring brought the back-breaking work of harvesting onions and radishes. It took a courageous and motivated person to enter an onion patch and look down long rows and rows of onions, but I was incredibly motivated. The process of bunching onions or radishes was arduous. I chose onions because they were easier to handle; radishes had rough leaves and had to be bound in bigger bunches than my twelve-year-old hands could manage. After school I would change clothes, walk to the onion field, pick up a bundle of 120 precut lengths of string, and tuck the bundle through the right belt loop of my jeans. The field boss would assign me to a row. It didn't take long to work out a system: I would straddle the row of onions, stoop down and pick a precise bunch, and slap the bunch against my leg with my left hand to knock off the dirt while with my right hand I grabbed one string from my belt loop and wrapped it twice around the bundle. Then it was simply a matter of tying a quick knot and dropping the bunch between the furrows. I had to repeat this process 120 times to earn fifty cents. Depending on how focused I was, I could earn between fifty and seventy-five cents an hour.

I *was* focused. Every morning, the five-mile school-bus ride took me past Nelson's Sporting Goods Store in St. George, with its display window full of softball gloves, bats, and balls. I always sat on the left side of the bus so I could look at those gloves as we passed the store. With that reminder each day, I was motivated to hurry to the onion patch every afternoon to bunch.

One morning, as the bus passed by the window, I decided to spend my lunch hour inspecting the gloves. As soon as the lunch bell rang, I raced the three blocks to Nelson's. Standing before the display, viewing the myriad gloves and inhaling their strong leather aroma, I felt an excitement in my soul that I still remember today.

At about eye level I spied one particular glove: a Wilson, with Billy Martin's signature on it. I envisioned myself with that glove on, catching a long fly ball out in left field. The price tag read $38.43. Too shy to try it on, I just eyed it—knowing with all my heart that this fielder's glove was the one for me. I returned to school, praying that I would be able to earn enough money.

After five solid weeks of bunching onions, working for two or three hours each day after school and all day on Saturdays, I finally had enough to buy the softball glove. I'll never forget the day I asked my mother if she would please drive me the five miles to the sporting goods store to purchase the coveted prize. I was holding the crumpled money in my onion-stained hand. She knew what I had done to earn it. Without hesitation, she smiled, "Yes, let's go."

As we walked in, my whole soul was aglow. I picked up my glove and put it on. It fit perfectly. Eye-level with the counter, I proudly counted out the $38.43, plus tax, in dollars and pennies. My mother wore a wonderful smile as I put the glove on my hand and floated out of the store.

As my mother drove me home, I scrutinized every inch of that glove: the light brown leather with Billy Martin's personalized autograph stamped in black, the bold "Wilson" brand across the wrist strap, and the words "Genuine Raw-Hide Leather" and "Snap Action" right in the pocket.

As perfect as the mitt seemed to me at that moment, I soon realized that the weeks of work that had gone into my purchase were just the beginning. Now the real training—of myself and my glove—commenced. To train the glove, I put my softball in it, tied some string around it, and began to form it. I slept with it, loved it, and kissed it. For my own training, I committed to daily practice of an hour or more. I had my sights set on being a pitcher, so to the side of the now-vacant "Dog House" I nailed a square piece of plywood that represented the strike zone. I stepped off my twenty-seven paces to the pitcher's mound, faced the target, and began my career.

The coach's phone call, announcing the start of spring practices, finally came. As we got into the season, I recognized immediately that I had a challenge ahead of me. The older girls, who had more experience and practice, were nearly always on the first string. Undaunted, I resolved that I was going to be a starter my first year, even though I was the youngest player on the team.

The night of the first game came. We gathered in the Dixie Sunbowl, the rodeo arena where all the Church softball games were played. As the first-string players were sent out onto the field, I was left sitting on the bench—praying with all my heart that somehow I would get the opportunity to go out and prove myself.

At the beginning of the eighth inning, I noticed a group of young men come into the arena. I also noticed that one young man kept looking at the left fielder. He would periodically wave at her to come toward him. She would just wave back and say, "I can't. I can't."

Finally, as the team ran off the field between innings, I saw him come over and talk to her over the railing. It appeared that he was trying to persuade her to leave with him. Under my breath, I was saying, "Go! Go!" If she went, maybe I would get to take her place. Sure enough, when the ump signaled our third out and our team was taking the field, I watched intently as the girl approached the coach to excuse herself. The coach turned, looked up and down the bench, and finally signaled for me to take left field. Fitting my new Wilson on my hand, I nodded to the coach and nonchalantly trotted out to left field—straining to keep my insides from exploding. I was sure that the bright arena lights were all celebrating with me.

It was the ninth inning; the score was 3–2 in our favor. The first batter hit a double over second base. Batter number two struck out. The third batter grounded out at first base, but the second-base runner advanced to third. Batter number four, their heavy hitter, confidently stepped up to the plate. The first pitch was a strike. The pressure got to our pitcher, because she followed with two wild pitches. The batter swung hard at the next pitch, but fouled it off.

From left field, the next pitch looked like a strike, but the umpire's call was "Ball three!" and we were on the brink of crisis—two outs, a runner on third, and a count of three and two.

As I looked at the stance of the batter, I instinctively dropped back and shifted to the right two or three feet. My sixth sense told me she was going for the left-field fence. I saw our pitcher wind up, then release; the batter swung, and the ball, sure enough, sailed high in the air, right past third base, deep into left field. Adrenaline took over. I raced for the baseline and, with a spectacular backhanded reach, caught the ball—right on the Genuine Raw-Hide Leather stamp. Though out of breath, I could still hear the roar from the crowd and the shout of victory from my teammates as they ran toward me. I met them with a big grin. "Hey, nothing to it!" My benchwarming career was over.

The years have come and gone, and my tired and worn Wilson glove, with the faint Billy Martin signature, has been retired to a shelf by my bedside. However, the glorious memory of desiring, working for, obtaining, training, and maintaining my glove lives on.

Caring and the Curling Iron

It was the day of Woodward Junior High's eighth-grade class assembly. I was in a crowd scene in the opening skit. We had been practicing for weeks; our goal was to win the award for the Best Class Assembly.

Before I left for school, my mother had painstakingly curled my hair. Her job was difficult for two reasons: first, my hair was absolutely curl-resistant; second, the method of curling hair was a laborious, one-curl-at-a-time technique that was quite tricky. The curling iron looked somewhat like modern ones, except that it had two wooden handles joined together to form a U shape. Squeezing the handles together opened the hair-clip piece, allowing my mother to roll the hair into a curl. Another minor difference: it wasn't electric. The U-shaped handles, just larger than the mouth of our coal-oil lamp's glass chimney, held the iron in place as it dangled above the flame.

My mother would use a comb to part my hair into small sections, then take the thin curling iron out of the lamp chimney to curl each lock. As she finished one curl, she would place the iron back in the lamp to reheat, prepare the next bit of hair, and repeat the process until my whole head was in ringlets.

Just before I left the house, I looked in the mirror to see my beautifully curled hair. As I walked the three blocks to the school-bus stop through the unseasonably damp February morning air, my friends commented admiringly on my hairdo. I loathed standing still as long as it took, so I let Mama curl my hair like this only for church or special occasions. But I glowed under the compliments.

Twenty minutes later, as I got off the bus, I half expected similar comments from other schoolmates but was greeted by quizzical looks instead. Puzzled, I went straight to the rest room. As I looked in the mirror, I gasped, "Oh, no!" The ringlets had wilted. Looking back at me was a sad face surrounded by a mass of straight, stringy hair. It didn't even look combed. I was totally embarrassed, realizing that the assembly was only two hours away. Tears welled up in my eyes.

I waited in the bathroom until the school bell rang, indicating that everyone would be in class, then sneaked up the long flight of stairs to the principal's office and asked to use the phone. With a shaky voice, I explained my story to my mother. She asked to speak to the principal. After only a moment, Mr. Frei hung up the phone with a chuckle and sympathetically instructed me go meet my mother at the Texaco station next to Dick's Cafe, where she worked. Then he put his arm around my shoulders and escorted me to the door. By the time I walked the three blocks to Texaco, my mother had already driven the five miles from Washington, lighted the coal-oil lamp, and had the curling iron heating on the countertop.

She gave me a comforting hug. "It's not as bad as you think,

Gail," she said. "Hop up here on the counter." I sighed in relief; my mother was there. Everything would be all right. Once again she transformed my hair into beautiful ringlets, then drove me back to the school. With my confidence back and my mother in the audience, my performance was supreme.

When I became a mother myself, I remembered the lesson of Mama's curling iron and how important it was that my mother cared about me enough to come when I needed her.

Patience and Persistence: A Lesson from a Cow

My family lived on a small farm. After the harvest, as winter approached, my father would have to seek work in the closest big city, Las Vegas, which was 135 miles away. Although I had other sisters, somehow I was the only one who knew how to milk a cow, so the outdoor chores fell to me. I didn't mind; milking a cow was a lot better than having to scrub out the oatmeal kettle.

It was a fabulous Friday afternoon, made glorious by the thought of no school the next day. On the five-mile bus ride home, my friends and I excitedly made plans to go to the latest picture show in town; the gang would meet at Abner's General Store at 6:00 P.M. Since I didn't get home from school until after 4:00 every day, this didn't give me much time to get all my chores done, get ready, and be back at the store at the appointed time.

I had to slop the pigs, feed and water the horses and chickens, gather the eggs, collect the wood chips to start the morning fire, and milk the cow. I hurried through the chores as quickly as I could, saving the milking for last. Finally, milk bucket in one hand and hobbles in the other, I walked into the corral. M.J.B., the cow, was lying in the far corner. She had earned her name by straining for the last morsel of oats and getting her nose caught in the M.J.B. coffee can my dad used for graining the cows.

I hurried toward her, anxious to get her up on her feet and moving toward the manger. She slowly levered up her back legs, then her tail, and awkwardly put her front feet under her. We then began the arduous journey toward the manger. It seemed that all my, "Yip, Yip," and "Hurry along!" encouragement did nothing but slow her down. She knew I was in a hurry.

Finally she reached the manger. I set my milk bucket down and quickly secured the hobbles by reaching in front of her back legs, placing the hobble on her left hock, bringing the chain across the front of her legs, and fastening it on her right hock. Being in such a rush, I didn't take the time to follow my usual practice of securing the tail inside the hobble. I pulled up the milking stool and sat down. Again, feeling time pressing, I didn't clean her udder and teats thoroughly, only briefly brushing away the hay and dried manure.

Placing my head in her flank, I glanced at my watch, only to be reminded of how little time I had left. Of course, as I began milking, M.J.B. refused to let her milk down. Her uncooperative attitude brought loud, impatient words from my mouth, and she answered with a stinging slap of the tail on the side of my head. I responded by pushing my head deeper into her flank and squeezing harder on the teats. She persisted in her stubbornness, shuffling forward, almost upsetting the milk bucket and knocking more debris off her udder into the pail.

I ran out of patience and shouted, "Okay, M.J.B., I've had it!" Grabbing the bucket in my right hand, I stood and swung it at her head. At that moment, she turned her head and caught the flying bucket with her horn, making a huge dent and a little hole three-quarters of the way up. M.J.B. had won the battle and left me facing an even greater crisis.

Now it wasn't just the time I had to worry about. If I quit at this point, I had to go back inside the house, face my mother with an empty milk bucket, and spend my evening at home. That prospect, along with the loss of the needed milk, was an unhappy one—not to mention the confrontation I would have with my dad, trying to explain the dented bucket to him when he returned home.

I knew exactly how much sympathy I would get when I explained that I was in a hurry because I wanted to go to a movie.

I knew what I needed to do. Taking a deep breath to calm myself, I spoke softly to M.J.B., rubbed her neck, and began again. When I settled down, the cow settled down, and I filled the bucket—to the hole. That day M.J.B. taught me a great lesson in patience. By the way, the picture show was great.

A leaf, a stem, and a brief root shooting down. I was learning at a very young age values and principles that would stay with me all my life. Honesty matters. God answers prayers. Working hard to achieve a goal brings success and satisfaction. Caring parents provide a stability greatly needed by their children. And patience and persistence can help a person concentrate on the process of work and find fulfillment in it. Focusing on only the desired product creates a rushed, impatient feeling and eliminates a great deal of the satisfaction that can come from work. I may not have known it then, but someday it would be important to me to be able to pass that heritage on.

A young trunk bending in the wind

4

In the 1970s, we were living in Portland, Oregon, and one of our children's favorite places to visit was OMSI, the Oregon Museum of Science and Industry. This marvelous facility provided numerous hands-on learning experiences for children and adults alike, such as an enormous model of a human heart with chambers large enough to walk through and "functioning" valves that visitors could touch, or a busy cross-section (behind glass) of a live, active beehive.

One display my children particularly enjoyed was called the "Love Machine." It supposedly measured the amount of love within the hearts of those who stepped up to the machine and placed their hands on the copper plates. Across the top of the display was a row of ten indicator lights, all of which would light up if the person was filled with love.

The first time we discovered this display, of course, my children were anxious to test their levels of love. One by one they took their turns standing up on the little step and placing their tiny hands on the plates. Each was pleased as he or she was able to turn on all ten lights, indicating an abundance of love.

After the initial interest had worn off and they moved on to other displays nearby, curiosity got the best of me and I decided to measure my capacity for love. Thinking that I was a naturally loving person, I confidently placed my hands on the copper plates. To my shock and chagrin, only five lights came on. Was the machine broken? I exerted more pressure on the plates, glancing around to be sure that none of my children were watching these bleak results. The harder I pushed, the more the fifth light flickered.

Somewhat put out, I removed my hands, wiped them on my pant legs, then tried again. Five lights. I was not only irritated, I was baffled as to why my children could produce ten lights and I couldn't. Words from the Bible, "and a little child shall lead them," rang in my ears. Considerably humbled, I trailed in their wake, realizing anew that children truly do lead—in love, in purity, in simplicity, in faith—and that sometimes the best thing an adult can do is follow their lead.

I later learned that what the "Love Machine" really measured was the moisture in hands. The more "loving" hands were those busy, sweaty little hands, not my cool, dry ones. However, that knowledge did not lessen the impact of the truth that had hit me so forcefully that day: children really do know an unconditional, all-encompassing love.

Children possess this natural love and an abiding faith in their parents, even when the parents forget about that unconditional trust. That's why they believe the terrible messages we sometimes send them in our tiredness or frustration: "You're careless. You're lazy."

That truth came home to me a few months ago when our twenty-two-month-old granddaughter, Shilo, was making a particular mess of herself in her high chair at the Sunday dinner table. Observing her food-caked face and hands, Hyrum, quite without thinking about it or meaning to do harm, said, "Look at you, Shilo! You're ugly!"

Shilo's sky-blue eyes welled with tears. Stacie, her mother, immediately came to her defense: "Grampy, you've hurt Shilo's feelings. She's not ugly; she's just messy."

Hyrum, realizing the message he had sent, quickly repented. Wiping her face and hands with a napkin, he said, "Shilo, you're beautiful. There's beauty under this messy face." Shilo beamed back at him.

If little Shilo, less than two years old, knew the difference between "ugly" and "messy," it seems obvious that a child's self-esteem begins to form at a very young age. A few unflattering words—even when spoken by someone who had provided lots of other previous evidence of love for Shilo—would have taken their toll if they hadn't been noticed and corrected.

But even for the most nurturing and loving parents, their children's teen years are generally a trial. Adolescent self-esteem is a roller coaster, and parents are not usually welcome on the ride. In the search for identity, most teenagers lose themselves for a while. They become clothes conscious, peer conscious, looks conscious, and self-conscious. Teenagers *do* need structure and parental direction, but they often resent being directly "taught." It takes all the proficiency, creativity, and ingenuity a parent can muster to quietly provide support, resources, and encouragement for good decisions.

The simple fact is that for most people adolescence is an emotional, ingenuous, and agonizing time when the parent and teenager alike endure "growing pains." My own teenage years were no exception.

Tomboy

As I struggled to learn how I fit in with the rest of the world, I grew to appreciate the counsel of David O. McKay, President of the Church during my growing-up years: "Be yourself, but be that perfectly." It was an often-uphill battle for me to realize that I was who I was, and that it was okay to be me. True self-esteem could come only by my recognizing that truth and working with it.

Due to my practice chasing cows among the tamaracks on the river bottom, I could speed down a 75-yard track in 9.2 seconds. I could balance a spinning basketball on the tip of my index finger, Harlem Globetrotters' style, besides handling the ball effortlessly and shooting with near-perfect accuracy. I could throw a softball from the right-field fence to get a base runner out at home plate.

Riding a horse—bareback or saddled—was heaven to me. God had gifted me with uncanny athletic talents.

As early as I can remember, I was labeled a tomboy. (Was my self-inspired nickname of "Tommy Boy Yell" a subconscious recognition of those qualities even at the age of four?) The tomboy label had no effect on me, however, during my grade-school years. My immediate classmates—one other girl and five boys—accepted me in either world. I could play rough-and-tumble with the boys at such games as cowboys and Indians, football, Annie-I-Over, and rubber guns. Or, when necessary (on cold, rainy days), I could be soft and gentle with the girls at such things as playing house, cutting out paper dolls, or painting pictures. My choice, however, was to be with the boys. It was a win-win situation because they needed me to make the teams even. Besides, I was a better player than any of them. I soon became their organizer, quarterback, pitcher, and floor general. The label "tomboy" was a small price to pay for six years of grade school glory.

The painful years came when the long yellow school bus hauled me to Woodward Junior High. Overnight, my beloved blue jeans and sweatshirts were relegated to home-only status by the new rules of the game: "Girls have to wear frilly dresses, black patent-leather shoes, and bows in their hair to school." The vision of my jeans left hanging on my bedroom doorknob—so I could jump right into them after school—helped me cope with the changes.

No longer could I be the athletic ace I had been in my grade school years. No longer could we all go out and play a game of football together at recess. It was a painful loss of identity for me to drop from reigning supreme to being unseen. The boys and girls were now separated. Boys went to wood shop; girls took home economics. The boys had their physical education classes and the girls had theirs. These were the 1950s; we were never to play together again.

My biggest frustration came when it was time to select the

school's basketball, baseball, or track and field teams. Girls' athletics hadn't even been born yet. It was difficult to sit on the sidelines and watch my male peers begin the journey of realizing athletic hopes and dreams that I too ached to fulfill. I felt the way my mom's homemade bread looked when she forgot to put in the yeast.

My physical education class became the highlight of my day. I couldn't understand why the majority of girls dreaded this class. It was my hour to shine, to get out of a dress, to breathe and be free. My gym class was a glimmer of fulfillment of my athletic abilities—that is, until Miss Marker entered my life in the ninth grade. I still wonder why she was hired as a physical education teacher. She did not fit my mental picture of a gym teacher, nor could she compare to the fun-loving and personable Miss Armstrong of the previous year, who would dress and join us in the sports we played each day.

Miss Marker was of medium build, with stiff, bleached-blonde hair that always looked professionally done. She wore thick, red lipstick, heavy eye makeup, and gaudy jewelry to match her expensive, fashionable clothing: colorful Jantzen sweaters and tight, knee-length skirts with coordinating four-inch heels. Seeing her walk down the hall was like watching a model on the catwalk at a fashion show. As she spoke in her low, indefinite voice, she would gesture with her hands to show off her long, painted fingernails, invariably colored to match her bright lipstick.

Miss Marker's mission was to instill in us poise and social graces. We did not change out of the dreaded dresses we wore each day to school. Rather, we met in the auditorium, where Miss Marker would lecture to us about the importance of walking, sitting, and carrying ourselves properly. She would then use the stage to demonstrate graceful mannerisms: how to ascend or descend stairs, how to get into or out of a car, how to walk and sit with correct posture, how to be seated at a table, how to stand and turn when modeling clothing. At that point in time, I could see no relevance in such things, though other girls were very enthusiastic about them.

The requirement for a satisfactory grade this particular term was to gracefully perform a modeling routine in front of the entire class. Each girl, individually, in a dress and high heels, had to walk up the stairs to center stage, face the audience, pose, make a full turn, pose again, and then walk over to a chair and properly seat herself. At this point, it was critical to hold the legs together, properly clasp the hands in the lap, and sit erect on the front portion of the chair. The final step was to stand, go around the chair, descend the stairs on the other side of the stage, and return to the audience. This performance horrified me.

As I think about it now, there were many factors increasing my tension. First of all, my clothes were all hand-me-downs. I was fearful of being compared to my better-dressed peers. Second, I had never worn a pair of heels in my life. I knew that I would look silly. Third, I felt uncomfortable about parading myself in front of others. Finally, I was terrified to stand alone and face those million eyes. My self-esteem could not cope with this demand.

The day came that I knew would bring my turn to take the stage. I entered the auditorium and sat on the back row of folding chairs, clutching my coat tightly about me, thinking that somehow it would go away, denying the reality that I would need to perform. Something would happen: maybe she would forget to call my name; maybe I could turn invisible; maybe, being on the back row, hiding behind the class, I would just be overlooked.

The number of girls who had not yet modeled became fewer and fewer, yet the slow-moving minute hand of the clock told me there were still twenty minutes left in class. Reality was closing in. As my inevitable turn drew closer and closer, a burning sensation shot through my body and I started to break out in a cold sweat. I couldn't handle it. I would *not* walk across that stage. Tears filled my eyes; I stood up, still bundled in my coat, and slumped out the side door. I would rather suffer the consequences.

I don't actually remember what those consequences were. Miss Marker may have lowered my grade from an "A" to a "B." It may have been the reason I did not receive the award some time later for "Girl Athlete of the Year." The really important consequences, however, went deeper. For example, in class, I would know the answer to a teacher's question, but the fear inside was so great I could not—and would not—respond. I couldn't stand before a class and give an oral report. As time went by, my inability to communicate and express myself deepened to a near-phobia.

Then senior high school began. Although the flavor of junior high frustrations lingered, high school introduced an intricate and intriguing challenge called the dating game. I soon discovered that maintaining a feminine image and disguising my athletic prowess among men took all the genius I could engineer. A "movie date" was safe, but being asked to play tennis forced an interesting decision. Should I play "like a girl" and lose, or really play as well as I could and take the chance of beating my date? I had to ask myself, "Do I want another date with this guy?" If so, I let him win. If not, I started looking around for another ride home. It was a painful time of juggling my desire to be *me* with my desire to be popular.

Prom Night

The junior prom was three weeks away. Among the girls, the exciting game of getting a date for the occasion had begun. That excitement was catching even me. Of course, the fact that my two best friends already had dates only elevated my motivation. Secretly, I had to admit that a certain brown-eyed, dark-haired boy who rode on my school bus already put a tickle in my stomach every time we passed.

I laid out my battle plan. First, I knew that I had to get his attention. I would have to wear the "right" clothes (frilly dresses and patent-leather shoes) and look perfect every day. I also needed to be discreet and nonchalant. I would have to research his interests. Did he like sports? What were his favorite teams? I hoped he was a

Celtics fan. Conversations about football, baseball, or basketball would be easy for me. I knew the stats of Mickey Mantle, and that Johnny Unitas was quarterback for the Baltimore Colts.

I would also have to play the detective to find out his routes, patterns, and daily schedule. Who were his friends? Where was his locker? Where and when were his classes? Where did he eat lunch and what was his daily path? I envisioned him descending the stairs just as I turned the corner and delicately placed my hand on the banister to begin my ascent. Mysteriously, at that very moment, my lace handkerchief would float to the floor at his feet. Of course, he would gallantly pick up the handkerchief and bow as he gently placed it back in my hand. "Your handkerchief, Mademoiselle." Timing was everything.

Of course, he would never notice that I was playing this game. I would be completely innocent and naive, though observant and complimentary. Discreet flattery wouldn't hurt either: "Nice shirt," or "What cologne are you wearing?" or "Good job on Mr. Frei's last test."

Monday morning, I launched my prom plan. I spent the first two days observing his every move. By Wednesday, I was able to position myself by his locker just as he happened to be exchanging his books between classes. "Oh, hi. How was your class?" I said as I casually breezed by, my palms sweaty. The play of the day happened as I rounded the corner by the stairs to begin my ascent just as he was reaching the landing coming down. He couldn't help but notice me. Perfect timing. I nonchalantly greeted him. "Oh, hello. Are you having a good day?" He stopped, and we spoke long enough for me to throw in a compliment about a new shirt he was wearing. The stair incident was crucial. He actually spoke to me. My plan was progressing nicely.

I continued my tactics daily, and the next victory occurred a few days later. I managed to brush by him in the bus line while talking to some of my friends nearby. At the same moment, a girl-friend of mine standing behind him called me over to talk about a homework assignment. Perfect setup. As we finished our discussion, the brown eyes turned around and the three of us began talking about last night's high school basketball game. He seemed pleasantly surprised that I was able to speak his language. We talked about the team's quick fast break, and that last-second baseline shot that won the game. The school bus came and the line dissolved too quickly, but during our conversation he had looked at me with different eyes. I knew I had made an impression.

The long-anticipated phone call finally came on a Friday night that I will never forget. I was in the living room, relaxing by the fire. My only thought was that school was out for the weekend. Mom was bustling around in the kitchen. When I heard the phone ring— one long, one short—I had a feeling it might be for me. That thought was confirmed when my mother announced, with her hand over the receiver, that I was wanted—by a baritone voice.

My heart began pounding in my throat as I struggled to get to the phone. I moved in slow motion; my legs seemed immobile, as in a dream I'd had when someone was chasing me. "Mustn't panic. Calm down, Gail!" This was the fruition of my plan, *the* phone call—the one I had been hoping for, working for, and praying for.

My acting career began. Without a tremble in my voice, I managed, "Hello?"

"Hi. This is Ron." (As if I didn't know.) "Gee, how are you doing?"

"Oh, I'm fine." (I was grateful he couldn't see through the phone.)

"What are you doing?"

"Oh, nuthin'."

"How's the weather down in Washington?" (We were only ten miles away.)

"Oh, fine. How's it out there in Leeds?"

"Fine. How did you do in Mr. Hafen's algebra class?"

"Oh, okay, I guess. It was a hard test." (I had flunked it, but I'd never tell.) "I bet you aced it, as usual."

"Yeah. I did okay."

Finally he asked the big question I had been waiting for: "Gail, would you go to the prom with me?"

My calm answer should have earned me an Oscar nomination. I said, "Well, let me check and make sure that I'm not doing anything that night."

I put my hand over the receiver and silently jumped up and down for a minute, then came back and reported nonchalantly, "That night is free. I'd love to go to the prom with you."

I don't remember hanging up the phone. I only recall running through the house, wildly announcing, "He asked me! He asked me! I have a date to the prom!"

Immediate preparation for prom night began. I had two weeks. For most, that was probably sufficient time, but for me, a tomboy unfamiliar with the process of shedding my comfortable Levi's for a formal gown, it would take every minute. The very thought of the transformation I had to undertake was frightening, but the decision had been made; there was no turning back.

My mother was the Queen Shopper. Her idea of shopping was to go to every store, try on every article of clothing, then return to the first store and purchase the first item she had tried on. In contrast, my mode of shopping, when the need arose, was to go to the store, find as quickly as possible what I needed—usually a pair of Levi's or a sweatshirt—and buy it. Thankfully, because St. George was then a small town, Mama's shopping maneuvers were limited. There were only two stores in which formals were sold: Snow's Dress Shop and Mendy's, across the street. We entered Snow's first.

We were greeted immediately by a saleswoman. When my mother explained our need, the saleswoman was happy to suggest several styles I might like. As I entered the stuffy dressing room with my first choice, I recall feeling uncomfortable exchanging my Levi's and sweatshirt for the strapless gown. When I stepped out to show my mom and the saleswoman, I kept wanting to wrap my arms around my neck to cover my bare shoulders. Despite their complimentary comments, I felt strange and was certain I looked funny too.

My style and size were not to be found at Snow's. The fresh air felt so good as we began our trek across the street to Mendy's. Once inside, we were again met by a helpful saleswoman, who pointed out a variety of dresses. As she was expounding the virtues of this or that gown, a sky-blue dress of tulle and taffeta almost jumped out at me from an obscure rack in the back corner. For the first time, I spoke up: "May I look at that one?" As she pulled the dress off the rack and held it up, lights flashed and cymbals crashed: This was the one. I excitedly took it to the dressing room to try it on. Blue was my favorite color—it matched my eyes. Though the dress was strapless, the tulle was arranged on the shoulders to give the modest look that I needed. My only concern at that moment was that it felt a little big in the chest. As this was my first experience with a strapless dress, I asked myself, "What keeps this thing up?" The saleswoman seemed to read my mind. "No problem," she said. "A few alterations, and this dress will fit perfectly." My mother agreed wholeheartedly. "Gail, you will be the princess of the prom. Now all you need are the accessories." The saleswoman, of course, was happy to direct us to the strapless bras, garter belts, and nylons, and suggested that we drop down the street to Center Clothing for the shoes to complete my ensemble. As we prepared to leave, without hesitation my mother pulled from her purse the cash she had earned waiting tables at Dick's Cafe. This was an extravagant price to pay for a one-time affair. Only years later did I realize the extent of her sacrifice.

The day of the big prom finally arrived. It took me all afternoon to prepare. Of course, the first priority was to wash my hair so Mama could roll it in curlers and then wrap it in a dish towel to set while I soaked in a long, hot bath with perfumed oil. The next step was to manicure my nails, then douse my body with all

the appropriate lotions, powders, creams, and perfumes. By this
time my hair was dry, and I sat on a stool while Mama coiffed it
and supervised my last-minute touches.

At last, it was time to put on my formal. The saleswoman was
right: it fit perfectly. As I stood and looked in the hallway mirror,
my mother came from behind and placed her treasured rhinestone
necklace about my neck. The tomboy disappeared (at least for
tonight); there in the mirror I beheld the princess of the prom.

The magic moment was broken by the timely knock on the
door. My mother answered and announced that Ron had arrived.
As I entered the room, my handsome date, dressed in a sharp-
looking black suit and tie, took a step toward me and handed me a
plastic bag with a beautiful, white-carnation corsage. I graciously
thanked him and gingerly pulled it out of the bag. My mother
stepped in to help; as she began to pin it on my dress, one of the
small carnations fell to the floor. Mama carefully picked it up and
reassured us that it would take only a moment to make it look as
good as new. She walked to the sewing machine, positioned in
front of the living-room window, and retrieved a straight pin, then
skillfully arranged and fastened the fallen flower. It was impossible
to tell which one she had replaced. The corsage looked perfect as
she pinned it to my tulle and taffeta formal. Ron put my coat
around my shoulders and we were off to the dance.

An hour of ecstasy passed. We waltzed to such love songs as
"The Tennessee Waltz," "Love Is a Many-Splendored Thing," and
"The Rock and Roll Waltz," intermingled with the more upbeat "Mr.
Sandman" and "Don't Be Cruel." We swung and turned, waltzed and
jitterbugged. I was totally in love. My game plan had worked, and
this moment was worth all the ingenious tactics I had employed to
be with Ron tonight.

As we whirled around and around, my eyes were at the same
level as all the men's lapels. It began to dawn on me that each lapel
bore a small flower. My body instantly and uncontrollably stiffened
in Ron's arms, and my palms broke into a cold sweat. Ron sensed

my emotion and must have perceived what I was thinking. "It's all right, Gail. It doesn't matter." Too late. The spell was broken. His words couldn't change the awful realization that gripped my heart: the flower that my mother had so painstakingly fastened to my corsage was . . . his boutonniere.

Moving On

The tragic ending to my prom date with Ron did not mar me for life. I dated him for a while, but the summer passed, and so did he.

In the fall, a new family moved into town. In Washington, where very little ever changed, this event became the talk of the town. My own interest was piqued because this family had a boy, Ira, who was just my age. We rode the same school bus every day. One Friday afternoon, on the bus ride home, we sat together. Amid all the excitement and chattering that accompanies the out-of-school-for-the-weekend atmosphere, Ira casually asked if I could go with him to the movies that night. He said that he would have to ask his mother if she could drive us and another couple of friends; then he would telephone me.

It was the first time I had ever been approached like that, so I walked home wondering if this was a date or just a friendly get-together. When I asked my parents if I could go, I told them that he had asked me out. Just to be safe, though, I broke into my piggy bank for enough nickels, dimes, pennies to cover the seventy-five-cent admission fee. My Levi's pocket was cumbersome with the change, but I wanted to be prepared.

About 6:00 or 6:30, the phone rang. Ira was calling to verify that he and his mother would be there to pick me up at 7:00. His other friends wouldn't be able to go. When they pulled up, Ira came to the door to get me, then led me to the rear door of the car. We got in the backseat, and his mother chauffeured us.

Upon arriving at the old Gaiety Theatre on Tabernacle Street in St. George, I remember getting out of the car and holding back

somewhat as we approached the ticket booth. I breathed a sigh of
relief as Ira held up two fingers and said through the glass window,
"Two, please." It was a bona fide date, all right. As we walked into
the movie house, I had to keep my hand on my pocket to silence
the coins I had robbed from my piggy bank.

The following spring, Ira's family moved back to Farmington,
New Mexico, but every summer Ira would come to stay with his
sister and her family in Washington. A group of eight or nine of us
would get together on those summer evenings to go to the movies,
play games in the park, "borrow" watermelons from Mel Adams's
patch, or attend the church youth dances and functions. Over the
next two summers Ira and I would hold hands, or he would put
his arm around my shoulder; during the school year we wrote letters and talked to each other on the phone. We had a good relationship, and I remember praying to know if he was the one I
should marry. But the last summer he returned, it was with another
girl. My heart wept—for a couple of days. Then my mother
reminded me that he would probably never be a Wyoming rancher.
My prayers had been answered again.

You see, ever since I had read the great classic cowboy novel
The Virginian as a young girl, I had fantasized that I would marry a
Wyoming rancher. I daydreamed about stepping out onto the
porch of our ranch house and surveying the surrounding mountains and our expansive ranch, with the corrals full of beautiful
horses. I could see myself on horseback, gathering the cattle or gal-
loping over the range toward the setting sun.

I don't recall when I first started to wonder about whom I
would marry. Would he be tall? Would he have blue eyes or
brown? I do remember that often, in my prayers, I would ask
Heavenly Father to help me recognize my dream cowboy when I
met him.

During my college years, first at Dixie Junior College and later
at Brigham Young University, relationships came and went. Each
association, being on a more mature and serious level than my

earlier relationships, required more fervent prayer when it came down to the decision-making time. In each case, circumstances and feelings told me this was not the one.

In the meantime, I was majoring in physical education and helping pioneer women's athletics. I thoroughly enjoyed the challenge of self-discipline, the ecstasy of athletic expression, and the thrill of victory that had returned to my life.

The crowning event of my Dixie College career occurred my first year there, when we were invited to participate in the first-ever Intermountain Collegiate Athletic Conference women's basketball tournament held at Brigham Young University in Provo, Utah. During the two-day tournament, we played against teams from the University of Utah, Utah State University, Westminster College, Brigham Young University, and Snow College. We played well in the tournament and found ourselves in the championship game with Westminster College.

With three seconds left in the game, the score was tied. The guard defending me fouled me as I was bringing the ball down the court. I remember looking up at the score board as I stepped up to the foul line: 17 to 17. I looked at my team and realized the championship was in my hands. I remember my heart beating a thousand miles an hour as I released the ball. It dropped through the hoop! We held out for the remaining three seconds and came back waving the victory flag.

This experience influenced my decision to go on to Brigham Young University with the same major. There I played on the women's basketball, softball, and volleyball teams. I set a university broad-jump record that held for eight years. Because of my speed, I was designated pacesetter for a world-champion runner training at the university for the next Olympics.

I had come through adolescence intact. During my university years, I finally became comfortable with who I was and what I could do with my life and my talents. Under those wonderful circumstances, graduation came all too quickly. That evening, as my name was presented, "A. Gail Cooper," a champion walked across the stage in front of thousands of eyes to receive the diploma: baccalaureate in the field of physical education. Beneath my traditional black graduation gown, I was wearing my beloved blue jeans.

5
A new limb strong

I have been in many schoolrooms, but a patch of arrow weeds in the river bottoms near my home was the place in which I received an education for eternity.

It was my first winter quarter at Dixie Junior College. I was dating a young man, Richard, from Cedar City, who was also attending Dixie. We would often double-date with Richard's first cousin, Wells Harrison. We had many good times together and came to know each other well. One Saturday night we had been at a dance together and thoroughly enjoyed ourselves. The next day, a friend called to tell me that Richard and Wells had been in an automobile accident. Richard was not seriously injured, but Wells had been killed.

I was stunned. What a fine line there was between life and death! I began to ask myself some sobering questions. Where was Wells now? Why did this have to happen? Why to Wells? Why now?

At Wells's funeral, a sermon given by Brother Tobe Hunt directly addressed the question of the meaning of life and death, as captured in the explanations of Alma. Though I don't remember the details of the talk, I do remember the feeling that penetrated my heart. I knew Brother Hunt had spoken the truth. I was comforted and left with a desire to read the Book of Mormon and find out more.

I had been given this book as a gift when I was a child. Many times teachers and friends had told me to read it, but I had never found it important until now. I went home and dusted off my unused copy. As I read, I became deeply involved in the account that unfolded from the pages. One particular king, instead of living off the labors of his subjects, worked with his own people and gave service to them. A charismatic military leader rallied his people to defend their freedoms in the face of a powerful enemy force. In another military battle, 2,000 young warriors showed great faith and were preserved from death. A prophet demonstrated great courage in testifying of a king's need to repent, even though it drove the king to burn him at the stake. Other parts of the story taught me the value of prayer, the actuality of Christ's resurrection, and the reality of my relationship with him. Most important, I learned that it was possible for my own weaknesses to become strengths through my faith in Jesus Christ.

I longed for the book not to end. I did not want to lose the new feelings inside me. Although I had grown up in a deeply religious culture, I was only now beginning to understand why great-great-grandparents had sacrificed family, friends, hometowns, and countries, faced incredible hardships, and endured the Dixie red sand and blazing sun to plant cottonwoods and mulberries for shade and shadowfall. I wanted to know for myself the truths my ancestors held precious.

I closed the book and walked down the road to the creek bottom about a mile below my house. There, in a childhood hideout screened by arrow weeds and willows, I knelt and prayed. The feeling that came over me could best be described as the warmth of the sun on a cool April day; it gently touched my neck and back and flowed down over and penetrated through me. When I left the willows, I knew for myself that there was a God, that he cared about me individually, and that he would help me overcome my fears and weaknesses.

After my experience in the arrow weeds by the creek, I had a strong desire to become closer to God through attending my church meetings and serving others. That experience and the feelings it generated created a spiritual foundation for my life that would stay with me ever after. I set goals to finish my education and then to go on a mission for The Church of Jesus Christ of Latter-day Saints—decisions that literally changed my life.

A Mission to England

My arrival in England as a new Mormon missionary was one of the great culture shocks of my young life. For a young woman from the vast expanses of the western desert, the closed-in environment of mists, rain, and clouds was oppressive. In the country around my hometown, cactus and sagebrush outnumbered people. Here I felt smothered by the press of people who spoke a different version of my native tongue than the one I knew. In contrast to the slow, leisurely life of a small town, everything in England seemed to be in a state of bustle, on the move.

There were six new missionaries in my group traveling to England that September day. We arrived at London's Heathrow Airport reeling from jet lag. As we deplaned amid the din of British dialects and multitudes of people hustling in every direction, it was a relief to spot two young men dressed in the familiar missionary attire. Elders Driggs and Bennett, assistants to the mission president, were there to welcome us, gather our bags, and give us a whirlwind tour through foreign, crowded streets as we made our way to the mission home, riding in the navy blue Thames van.

After a day of shifting my biological clock eight hours forward and being oriented to missionary duties and responsibilities, I was assigned to serve in the city of Harrow Weald in the northwest suburbs of London. In these new quarters, my biggest adjustment was dealing with the lack of open space. I had come from miles of wide-open grazing and farming land to kilometers of tightly connected, two-story housing rows; I felt claustrophobic. My only links to home were in looking up at the spacious, blue sky on an intermittently clear day, and in hearing the drone of airplane engines overhead, a reminder of how I arrived in England and how I would one day return home. Gradually, the homesickness faded as I began to serve the English people and to understand their language and culture. My first companion, Sister Belcher, was a great trainer, so it didn't take long to build my confidence in my ability to do missionary work.

Together Sister Belcher and I spent most of our waking hours trying to share our beliefs with the English people. Rain or shine, heat or cold, we were expected to be up at 6:00 A.M. and out on the street by 9:00 A.M., knocking on doors, talking with people on the streets, and generally being about the business of finding those who were ready to hear our message. Even though days could be long and discouraging, there were the wonderful times when someone would actually invite us in, listen to the message, feel the Spirit, and go on to become converted.

After serving in Harrow Weald for two months, I received a phone call from the mission president, Preston Robinson, saying that I was to be transferred to another city, Harlow New Town. Firsts always leave lasting memories. I was saddened to leave my first companion, my first (now familiar) area, and my first English friends. I would be starting all over again.

On November 21, transfer day, the blue Thames van pulled up to collect me and my belongings. Homesick already, I took a last look at my familiar surroundings and said good-bye to my companion and landlady. I was then taken to the mission home in the heart of London, some forty-five minutes away, along with all the other missionaries being transferred that day. Here, the missionaries and their baggage would be loaded into different vans and sent out to their new areas.

It was a foggy, cold, dark evening, about 6:00 P.M. Coming from sunny St. George, I was not yet acclimated to the misty, biting, English air. As I walked out of the mission home, I was bundled up in three sweaters, a heavy coat, a scarf, a hat, gloves, and near-thermal nylons. I looked like a refrigerator box as I awkwardly boarded the outgoing van.

Before I took my seat, I quickly scanned the other missionaries to see who was being transferred to my new area. Straining to see through the darkness, I did a double take at the occupant of the left rear seat. In a flash, my childhood fantasy appeared before me: a handsome cowboy in a white, ten-gallon hat, a colorful western shirt, buckskin cowboy boots, and chap-covered Levi's. His belt bore a huge, silver buckle, displaying a fierce golden eagle in flight. He stood proudly, with his thumbs hooked in his front pockets. There was a shiny, silver-barreled, ivory-handled six-shooter in the holster on his right hip, and a lasso in his deerskin-gloved hand. The Virginian! The man of my dreams.

I blinked and looked again. This time I saw a tall, dark-haired missionary in regulation suit and tie. He was thrillingly handsome, however, and my earlier impression stayed with me. *Oh no, I* thought. *Not here; not now. I made the commitment to be here as a missionary. I shouldn't even be having these thoughts.* I desperately brushed all feelings aside as I settled back in my seat for the drive.

While we were traveling to our new area, I found out that the left rear seat was occupied by Elder Hyrum Smith. Elder Smith was going to Cambridge, an hour's drive beyond my destination of Harlow. When our zone leader dropped us off, he informed Sister Booth, my new companion, and me that a week later the entire mission would be meeting in the town of Crawley to celebrate an American Thanksgiving. He would pick us up at 6:00 A.M.

A week later we climbed in the van and started the lengthy process of picking up the other pairs of sisters and elders in our district. As we approached Cambridge to pick up Elder Smith and his companion, I could not deny feeling excited to see him again. When he got in the van, I felt a flutter for this young man—a feeling that I quickly suppressed.

During the four-hour drive to Crawley, the eight of us (two sisters and six elders) had a great time exchanging stories about the missionary work in our areas and about the experiences we were having in a foreign land. As usual, our minds drifted toward home and we talked about the different Thanksgiving traditions we were missing. In the course of the conversation, I learned that Elder Smith would finish his mission in March, that he was from Hawaii (downtown Honolulu), that his parents were schoolteachers (not ranchers), and that he had ridden a horse only once in his whole life. Somehow, this news did not alter my feelings for him; with an eye of faith, I saw in him the kind, open, and charismatic traits of my Virginian. I didn't know how, but I knew that somewhere, sometime, the cowboy of my dreams would emerge in Elder Hyrum Wayne Smith.

Despite the strength of those feelings, I managed to keep my focus on missionary work. As the new year began, Sister Booth and I were approached by our landlord. He wondered, "You two spend all day talking to people on the streets and knocking on doors throughout Harlow New Town. How come you've never knocked on our door to share your message with us? What are you telling these people?" Amazed at his questions, Sister Booth and I exchanged dumbfounded glances. Needless to say, he didn't have to ask twice. We immediately set up an appointment and began sharing our message with the Woolridge family.

A week later, Sister Booth received that unexpected telephone call from President Robinson; she was being transferred. Sister Dutson, one of the missionaries who had traveled to England with me, would be taking her place. Sister Dutson and I continued working with the Woolridges, and shortly thereafter the entire family accepted our message and were baptized members of the Church.

It was mid-February when we received yet another surprising call from President Robinson. He explained that we were being called as "traveling sisters." He and Sister Robinson had just completed a missionwide tour and felt that there was a need for experienced leadership in various Relief Society programs. Our purpose was to travel to designated branches and strengthen the Relief Societies by teaching leadership skills. It took us two or three days to close our affairs in Harlow New Town, notify our landlord, and pack our belongings for our new headquarters, the mission home in London.

Upon arriving, we were given a day of instruction by Sister Robinson, who had been asked by President Robinson to head this work with the various branch Relief Society programs. We were told that our first assignment would be in Norwich, one of the northernmost cities within the mission boundaries. That evening, as we went downstairs to get into our assigned car—a sporty Triumph sedan, the envy of all the missionaries—the president's assistants came running out. "Sister Cooper! Sister Dutson! We have had a change of plans. Instead of going to Norwich, President and Sister Robinson feel impressed that you are needed in the Southend Branch."

We went back inside to get acquainted with the new plans. We would be working with the Southend district leader to boost branch morale and assist in building leadership. The assistants explained to us that they had already notified the district leader in Southend of this change. By the time we arrived, he would have arranged a place for us to stay. With new maps in hand, we sped off in our Triumph to our new assignment.

When we arrived, we were met by the district leaders, none other than Elder Hyrum Smith and his companion, Elder Jensen. Elder Smith explained that he had originally made arrangements for us to stay with the family of the branch president, but he had just received a distressed phone call saying that their young children had come down with the chicken pox. On such short notice, the only other place he could find for us was in a flat next door to the legendary Sister Kinch, the landlady of the apartments where two sets of Southend elders lived. Under these circumstances, our meals would be provided by Sister Kinch, and we would eat with the elders in her flat.

We were soon to discover what an honor it was to be one of Sister Kinch's missionaries. A convert to the Church, she had housed missionaries for more than ten years and had a picture of each missionary who had stayed there on her Missionary Hall of Fame picture board.

The next morning, according to Sister Kinch's house rules, we sat down to breakfast at 7:30 sharp. Elder Smith was sitting directly across the table from me. I couldn't believe this coincidence—or was it perchance more than a coincidence? Here I was, sitting across the breakfast table from my dream. I tried to make interesting conversation about our missionary work and ask for suggestions about what we could do to help strengthen the branch, but I struggled with every word that came out of my mouth.

When we had finished eating, Elder Smith propped his elbows on the table and lightly clasped his hands together in front of his chin. My eyes were drawn to his handsome hands. They were strong yet refined, with long, slender fingers. On his right pinky finger he wore a gold ring bearing his initials. These were not the hands of a rancher, yet I found myself falling in love with them. I struggled to mask the emotions that involuntarily surfaced, thinking, *This can't be happening now. Not to me. I have a year left on my mission and he's going home in three weeks.* My faith weakened. Would we ever meet again? My thoughts were interrupted by Sister Kinch's stern but loving command: "It's time to get to work, lads and lassies." I was glad to breathe the cold, fresh air.

By the end of the week, hiding my feelings became more and more difficult. I felt an urgent need to avoid any nonmissionary encounter with Elder Smith. This meant eating dinner somewhere other than Sister Kinch's flat. I convinced Sister Dutson of my sudden, overwhelming craving for English fish and chips, and we conveniently ate out every night.

Yet because the two companionships were partners in the common cause of strengthening the branch, Sister Dutson and I had to work very closely with Elders Smith and Jensen. I found myself struggling increasingly to disguise my feelings. Therefore, I looked forward to the weekly reprieve from this situation provided by our returning to the mission home for preparation day.

We used these rest days (Mondays) to refill our physical and spiritual buckets after a long, regimented work week and a particularly taxing Sabbath. Sundays were always intense physical and spiritual experiences, from early morning until late night. Missionaries were expected to attend presidency meetings, preparation meetings, and all the auxiliary meetings as well as the regular church services. We were also always on call in case a teacher was ill or out of town; we often had to teach lessons or speak at the last minute. Of course, we brought our investigators to church and did our best to make them feel welcome in their new surroundings. We wanted to introduce them to members and be available to answer any questions they might have.

On Sunday evenings, we could count on at least one fireside or devotional for the youth, new members, or general membership. We often had to travel great distances by bicycle, train, or bus to get to these meeting places, and it was not uncommon for a missionary to be the main speaker. Indeed, in the eyes of the people, a missionary was invincible, the solution to the problem, the answer to the question, and the epitome of perfection. Attempting to fulfill such expectations required hours of preparation and incredible energy. Thus, Mondays were a welcome opportunity to rejuvenate ourselves and catch up on such things as doing laundry, writing letters home, or gathering with other missionaries to visit historical sites or take in London's cultural events. Sister Dutson and I also used Mondays to report our week's efforts to Sister Robinson.

Such a reprieve was my first Monday away from Southend. It gave me the chance to evaluate what was happening in my head and heart concerning Elder Smith. In these silent moments of thought I asked myself: Hadn't he been more attentive to me than the others in some of our conversations? Hadn't he waited for me at the meetinghouse door to open it for me and my companion and make sure, in his words, that we got home safely? Wasn't he always standing within sight of me in social gatherings—or was I standing within sight of him? Were these feelings one-sided?

Honolulu, Hawaii, was thousands of miles away. A year yet to serve was 8,760 hours of time. St. George, Utah? He probably had never heard of the town. The whole idea was an impossible dream. I turned my questions toward heaven. At that moment, a voice spoke inside my head: *Gail, Elder Smith is the man you are going to marry.* I couldn't disbelieve, but I was stunned.

On Tuesday, Sister Dutson and I returned to Southend to begin our missionary efforts anew. More cautious than ever in my associations with Elder Smith, I accomplished more that week than I had my entire mission, it seemed. Working hard caused Sunday night to come quickly. As we were about to leave for the mission home, Elder Smith came by with a message that we (Smith, Jensen, Cooper, and Dutson) had been asked to spend our preparation day helping an elderly missionary couple move from their "digs" in Cambridge to the mission home in London. To say no was unthinkable.

Though this excursion was duty bound, I felt that heaven had intervened to bring it about. Besides, I was legally allowed to throw on my sweatshirt and jeans, a happiness I had not enjoyed in many months. By 8:00 A.M. we had loaded the van with boxes, brooms, rags, and cleaning supplies and begun our journey to Cambridge, with Elder Jensen driving. Through the bright morning sunshine, itself a rarity, we wended our way over the English countryside. Crocuses bloomed in the patchwork of greening fields.

In this relaxed atmosphere, we talked, laughed, and philosophized. As we visited, I learned about the passing of Elder Smith's father the previous August and about the difficult decision he had made to remain in the mission field, rather than go home to attend the funeral. He then told me about his mother, who had strongly supported his decision, and I felt the great love and admiration he had for her. I learned that he had played center on his high school basketball team. "I was the tallest, of course, being the only haole among the Hawaiians," he laughed. He spoke of his plans for after he returned home from his mission. He would go back to Hawaii to spend some time with his mother, then enroll at the University of Utah for summer quarter.

I told him about the farm I grew up on in Washington, Utah, that I was one of five girls, and that I enjoyed riding, shooting, and even milking. My family had recently moved to nearby St. George and my parents were currently owners and operators of a nursing home, "Cooper's Rest Haven." I also mentioned that I enjoyed playing ball, but cautiously kept details of my athletic ability to myself.

At the Cambridge apartment, the elders packed and loaded the elderly couple's belongings while Sister Dutson and I cleaned the house. We completed our assignment and were back at the mission home by 2:00 P.M. Elders Smith and Jensen unloaded the van, then went about their business while we returned to our third-floor home base to begin our preparation-day activities. We started our laundry, then wrote letters home. I was on my way to the post office, just a block away, when Elder Smith, driving the van, pulled up beside me. He told me he was getting ready to return to Southend and reminded me that he would be going home next week. Then, out of the blue, he asked me if I would write to him. My answer was inspired. I lightly replied, "Hey, if I get a letter from you, I'll write back." He came back with, "It sounds like a plan," then drove off down the street. There was hope!

Elder Smith's final day in Southend arrived. Sunday he said farewell to the branch members and Sister Kinch; then Sister Dutson and I, along with Elder Jensen, gave him his last ride to the mission home in our Triumph. The mask I wore this day gave no indication of the turmoil that was raging within my head as well as in my heart.

This Monday was not only preparation day, it was also a transfer day. The mission home was bustling with missionaries who were there to be transferred or to pick up new companions. Transfer days were especially enjoyable because we were able to reunite with missionaries we had labored with in other districts.

They would share the most recent news about friends from our old areas, people we hadn't seen for weeks or months.

By midafternoon, all the missionaries who were scheduled for changes had arrived. We stood about in small circles of friends and former companions, talking and laughing together in the large reception area of the mission home. From the corner of my eye, I could see Elder Smith chatting with Elder Dyson, his companion for the day, in another circle of missionaries. At one point I thought I saw them simultaneously glance at me. Seconds later, Elder Dyson encouragingly patted Elder Smith's shoulder and nodded in my direction. Elder Smith stepped away from his group and purposefully walked toward me, breaking through my circle of missionaries as he approached. Facing me squarely, he said, "Sister Cooper, when all the missionaries have returned to their areas, Elder Dyson and I would like to visit with you and Sister Dutson in the Blue Room." At that instant, my heart could have used a pacemaker, but I managed to reply calmly that we would be there.

My mind conjured up a thousand thoughts. Why would Elder Smith want to talk to me? I knew he had worked in Southend for a total of thirteen months and had developed some close ties. I knew he had been sent there this second time to help the branch with some of the same challenges for which I had been called to help. Maybe he wanted to discuss developments in the Southend branch and tell me what I needed to do—or shouldn't do. Surely there were a dozen ordinary reasons why Elder Smith would want to talk to me.

A short time later, a group of missionaries decided to catch the red, double-decker bus and go out to dinner at Piccadilly Circus. Elder Smith was in that group, and he made a point of asking me specifically if I were going. Of course I didn't let on to him, but if I hadn't planned on going before, believe me, I was planning to now.

After an enjoyable but uneventful dinner, Sister Dutson and I returned to the mission home in time to see the departing missionaries board the Thames vans. We anxiously waited for the dust to settle in the reception area, just adjacent to the formal sitting room we called the Blue Room. On several occasions, just as it got quiet, a missionary would frantically burst back through the mission home doors to retrieve a forgotten umbrella or set of scriptures or raincoat. Finally the mission home was still, and Sister Dutson and I walked to the elegant Blue Room to await Elder Dyson and Elder Smith.

As we heard footsteps approaching, I knew that the answer to my question was just around the corner. We stood to greet the two elders with the usual handshake as they walked into the room. I reached across to shake Elder Dyson's hand first, then extended my hand to Elder Smith, who by that time was standing directly in front of me. Elder Smith took my hand and held it firmly, looked me straight in the eye, and said these very words, "Sister Cooper, I think I am falling in love with you. I'm going to Paris for three days to visit my Uncle Gene. I would like you to fast and pray about this, as I will be doing, and upon my return I would like to meet with you to see if you are feeling the same way I am."

Elder Dyson had apparently been prepared for this conversation, but not so my companion. Sister Dutson, a very poised and proper person, completely lost her composure. Her mouth gaped and she staggered back into the chair she had been sitting on. For me, although his words came as a total shock, they confirmed all my feelings for this man. He *was* the man I would marry.

For what seemed a long time, I was speechless, but I finally managed enough voice to reply that I would fast and pray about this surprising turn of events and that I looked forward to meeting him in the Blue Room in three days. I don't remember when our handshake ended, or how Elders Smith and Dyson left the room, but I do recall pulling Sister Dutson up from the chair and dragging her to the "lift" to ascend to our quarters in silence. I began my fast immediately.

I woke earlier than usual the next morning, trying to process the events of the previous day. I felt very warm inside as I re-created the conversation in my mind. Miracles really do happen. God really does answer prayers. I still couldn't believe the whole situation, but in retrospect I recognized that, from the first time I had seen him as my "Virginian" and through all our encounters, Elder Smith had been having the same emotions about me as I had been having about him. As the day proceeded, I found it difficult to concentrate on the work. Sister Dutson would have to pull me through today—but she wasn't much better than I. She was still recovering from the way Elder Smith had boldly presented himself the night before.

By the end of the third day, I knew that Elder Smith would indeed become a part of my life. When he returned from France, again we met in the Blue Room—accompanied, of course, by Sister Dutson and Elder Dyson. Interestingly, they didn't stand within hearing distance this time. Elder Smith shared with me his experience while in France visiting his uncle. More specifically, he told me of the three-mile walk he took along the Seine River from the Louvre to the Eiffel Tower, contemplating his feelings about us. Then he presented me with a beautiful blue-and-white silk scarf he had purchased from a roadside vendor at the end of his walk. He told me he knew of a surety that I was the one for him.

I related to him that I too had felt a peaceful assurance about our relationship. Sharing these emotions alleviated the heavy burden I had carried from stifling my feelings for so long. I was happy to tell Elder Smith that I knew he was my heavenly find. He told me he would write and send me his address as soon as he arrived home. Thus ended our Blue Room conversation.

That afternoon, through cleverly controlled circumstances, Sister Dutson and I included ourselves in the entourage that took Elder Smith and the other departing missionaries to the airport. I have to admit that I couldn't stifle the wistful twinge I felt watching his plane fly off for the Hawaiian horizon.

Despite my efforts to remain busy with the missionary work,

the days passed slowly as I anxiously awaited my first letter from Hyrum. By the end of three weeks, with still no word from him, I was beginning to wonder. Sister Dutson didn't help. Teasing, she would say, "Well, he probably waited for you at least a week. By now, a beautiful Hawaiian girl has a plumeria lei around his neck."

Finally, in the wee hours of the morning, the telephone rang on our floor and I was summoned to take the call. "I haven't heard from you. Is everything okay? How come you haven't written me?" His concerned voice sounded wonderful to my sleepy ears.

I responded, "Because you haven't written to me. I'm waiting for an address."

He said, "You mean you haven't received any mail from me?" He told me he had written as soon as he had returned home and was worried sick because he hadn't heard from me.

He was still waiting for me! I began to breathe a bit easier.

That afternoon the mission secretary handed me a battered, crinkled envelope with H W. Smith on the return address. The four-cent stamp told the story: This letter had come by boat instead of airmail. The next morning I scraped together two pounds, sixteen shillings, and headed to the telegram office. "RECEIVED YOUR LETTER STOP WILL WRITE TODAY STOP WITH LOVE STOP SISTER COOPER."

After this scare, I thought, *There's got to be some way to ensure that my Elder Smith will be kept safe until I return home.* After some days of thought and prayer, I asked Heavenly Father to preserve him until I got home, and promised myself that in return, I would be the best missionary England ever saw. I began to keep my commitment. A few weeks later, I opened a letter from Hyrum (he was no longer "Elder Smith") in which he told me that just as he was about to leave Hawaii to attend the University of Utah, he had received a letter from Uncle Sam drafting him into the United States Army. I didn't dare tell him that it was the answer to my prayers.

Lassoed

A short time later, I addressed an envelope with my best penmanship to Mr. and Mrs. Evan Erastmus Cooper. I carefully licked the Queen Elizabeth sixpence stamp and placed it on the appropriate corner. As I began to seal the flap, my anxieties about the news this letter bore told me I'd better read it just one more time. Carefully unfolding the lined notebook paper, I began:

> *Dear Mom and Dad:*
>
> *You'd better sit down to read this letter. I just sent off to Honolulu, Hawaii, the man I'm going to marry. His name is Hyrum Smith (of course, I know him as "Elder"; don't worry, Dad). I'm excited for you to meet him. He will be driving through St. George in the near future and will contact you before he gets into town. I'm sure that he can tell you the full story much better than I could in this letter.*
>
> *The work is still progressing well. I'll send a more detailed letter later.*
>
>

Love,

Your daughter of the Misty Isles,

Gail
>

As I refolded the letter, stuck it in the envelope, and licked the flap to seal it, I couldn't help but chuckle about how Mom and Dad would react when they read the news. They would wonder what had happened to their "Misty Isle" missionary (as Mom liked to refer to me in her letters). A few weeks later I received this response:

> *Dear Gail,*
>
> *Your Elder Smith paid us the promised visit. I let him sleep in your room. I overheard your dad saying to him, "If you are going to marry my daughter, then you better know something about her." Your dad then proceeded to take him upstairs and show him your guns and the gun case you made to house them, all the time telling story after story of your shooting expertise. After that, Dad drove him to Washington to show your Elder Smith your horses. He explained to him how you had broke them to ride.*

Elder Smith did not know what it meant to break a horse to ride. Although your dad was amazed at Elder Smith's lack of horse sense, he gave a detailed description of the meaning. Dad ended the afternoon with a historical tour of Washington, St. George, and the red hills of the surrounding area.

While they were on this expedition, I fixed a pot of beans and a batch of homemade bread so it would be ready when they got home. He seems like a fine fellow.

I miss you and love you,
Mama

P.S. Your dad noticed, when we were at the supper table, that he had no calluses on his hands.

As I read her letter, a little knot formed in my stomach. My dad, in an effort to brag about his tomboy, could be rough on a guy. I wondered how my Honolulu cowboy had handled my farm folks and our country lifestyle. I worried that my dad's behavior would cause Hyrum to have second thoughts about me. But time would tell. I had a mission to fulfill.

6
I answered

March arrived, and I said good-bye to England. The sky, which had always been my link to the wide-open spaces of home, was all around me. For some seven hours on the flight home I reminisced about the magnificent experience I had lived the past eighteen months. I had kept my promise to God, and God had kept his promise to me. Elder Smith was waiting for me.

Finally the captain announced, "Fasten your seat belts. We will be landing at O'Hare Airport in Chicago in fifteen minutes." As the plane descended and touched down on the runway, I looked out the window to see an enormous American flag waving in the March breeze. Tears welled in my eyes and a lump swelled in my throat. I was home.

A few hours later, I was in the arms of my family. My little sisters had grown; my dog, Mopsy, had died; the horses were waiting for me to ride; the garden needed to be planted; and my room was just as I left it. "Did you bring me anything from England?" "Can we help you unpack your bags?" The house was filled with excited chatter.

Suddenly the phone began ringing. It was Hyrum! How did he know that I had just walked through the door of my St. George home? The magic hadn't stopped. "I'm so glad that you're home," he said. "How was your trip? I'm looking forward to seeing you. When will your homecoming be?" I explained that the homecoming report was scheduled for Sunday, two days away. He told me that he was hoping to get leave from his base in Fort Ord,

California, so that he could come see me the next weekend. As I listened to his voice, that tingling, warm feeling began again, washing over my whole body. I was still in love.

Later that night, as we were all preparing for bed, the phone rang again. My mother answered it, then quietly retreated to her bedroom to talk on the extension. A couple of minutes later she returned to hang up the kitchen phone and nonchalantly finished closing down the house for the night. I thought it a little odd, but being travel weary, retired to my room without thinking much about it.

My body, adjusting to its new time schedule, demanded that I sleep late on Saturday morning. When at last I began the day, I noticed strips of notebook paper attached to doorways, walls, bathroom mirrors, beds, and the kitchen sink. Each message, written in my mother's handwriting, said, "To be forewarned is to be forearmed."

"Mom, what is going on?" I demanded.

She laughed nervously and answered emphatically, "Don't ask any questions. Just don't ask any questions. Read the notes." My mother was like an iron bar when it came to breaking confidences. I knew she was trying to warn me, but of what, I knew not.

Sunday was my missionary homecoming. The house was filled to capacity with friends and old companions from out of town. It was still early. In a general state of disarray, all the girls were gradually moving through the various stages of getting dressed. We all jabbered excitedly from room to room as we caught up on months of missed news. Friends were bursting with questions about my mission, and I had a lot of catching up to do about their lives, but always the conversations turned to inquiries about my Elder Smith. "Who is he? How in the world did you meet him?" I just quietly smiled. Where could I begin? It was impossible to tell the story.

For a missionary, the homecoming is the grand finale. I was nervous about talking to all these people, yet excited to share my mission experiences. As I was mulling over what I would say, my thoughts were interrupted by the telephone. It was Hyrum, and I could tell this was not a long-distance call. I said, "Hyrum, you sound very close."

He replied, "I am close. I'm calling from the Twin Oaks Motel. I'll see you in a minute."

The Twin Oaks Motel was about a block away. As I hung up the phone, pandemonium broke out. My mother, the iron bar, just shook her head and repeated, "To be forewarned is to be fore-armed." Apprehension seized me. I hadn't seen Hyrum since the mission field. I had been home only forty-eight hours, so I was still in the missionary frame of mind. How should I greet him? With a handshake? With a hug? Should I run out to meet him, or be wait-ing inside for his knock on the door? The assembled family and friends were free with their counsel, but before I could decide, he drove up.

As he got out of the car, I saw that he was in full Class A mili-tary uniform. Placing his hat on his head, he proceeded confidently up the front walk. The decision was made for me; someone opened the door and I walked out into the waiting arms of Hyrum Wayne Smith.

Somehow Hyrum had managed to obtain an extended week-end pass to come see me and attend the homecoming. As I walked in with "the" Elder Smith proudly in tow, the house that moments ago had been full and noisy was now silent and empty. A magician couldn't have performed a better disappearing act. Where were my loyal friends when I really needed them?

The homecoming was a treasured experience. After sacrament meeting, we assembled at home to enjoy Mom's superb roast beef with potatoes and gravy. All afternoon, friends, relatives, and assorted well-wishers dropped in to welcome me home. Finally, after the repast and repose of the weary, we were alone. Hyrum suggested that we take a drive so I could show him some of my favorite night highlights of St. George. I asked him if he wanted to see them all at once or one at a time. His answer, "All at once!"

Many towns have an elevated lookout point from which the surrounding area can be seen. In Tucson, Arizona, "A" Mountain provides the well-lit desert view; in Honolulu, Hawaii, the city lights from Tantalus enthrall night lovers. St. George, however, has *two* heights from which to view the area: the black ridge (near the airport) on the west, or the red-sandstone ridge on the north. My favorite lookout is the latter, Red Hill, topped by a large sandstone monolith, the Sugar Loaf. During the day, this red ridge offers a mile of different points along the rim from which to see the panorama of tall red mountains stretching to touch blue sky or the sunburned Virgin River winding through the green quilt of fields. Then, when day succumbs to night, the scene lights up and shows another picture. The strands of street lights, strung north and south or east and west, outline perfect glimmering squares. The tabernacle, chiseled from blocks of red sandstone, is the foundation of the steeple clock, which shows its face and hands in every direction. The white temple, brilliantly lit against the night sky, keeps darkness at bay with its ethereal glow.

The stars added their sparkling beauty as we stood holding hands, feasting upon this night scene. I could tell Hyrum was awed and impressed by this magic Dixie expanse.

"My feelings haven't changed, Gail."

"Nor have mine," I whispered, as he pulled me close for our first tender kiss.

We had just one more day to share two full lifetimes of experience. Monday morning I found my beloved Levi's in the same drawer I had left them in some nineteen months earlier. My dad walked us to the truck, describing where I could find all the saddles, bridles, ropes, currycombs, and brushes. He cautioned me that it was spring and that the horses had been ridden little during the winter. "They'll be a bit spunky, especially Chubby," he said. "You'd better not put Hyrum on Chubby."

"Thanks, Dad," I said, and we drove off to the pasture where the three horses were grazing.

Of course, the horses were in the farthest corner of the field. Taking the bridle and a rope, I told Hyrum to wait by the barn, then walked through the gate toward the horses. I think my own horse, Blaze, remembered me; at least he let me walk up to him. Not so with the others. They galloped to the other end of the pasture. I slipped the rope around Blaze's neck, put the bridle on, then grabbed a fistful of mane and swung up on his bare back. It was as if I had never been gone.

At a gallop, I headed toward the other two horses, rounding them up into the corrals. Dismounting and tying Blaze, I tossed Hyrum a currycomb and asked him to brush down my horse while I bridled Chubby. This was all so natural to me, I completely forgot that Hyrum had had almost no experience with horses.

I wanted Hyrum to have a positive ride, so I picked out our best saddle for him to put onto what I considered to be our best horse: Chubby. I showed him how to saddle Chubby by first looping and tightening the front cinch, then buckling the back cinch. Then I watched as he put on Blaze's saddle.

After I gave Hyrum a basic lesson with the reins, with particular emphasis on stopping the horse, we began our ride. As we headed for the river bottom, although Chubby was fresh, he seemed to be behaving himself. I relaxed and began to wonder why Dad had seemed so concerned. We rode along, enjoying each other's company. Suddenly, a gust of spring wind blew a tumbleweed right under Chubby's belly. He didn't buck, but crow-hopped and whirled around to get away from the weed. Hyrum managed to hang on like a professional while settling Chubby down at the same time. My Virginian couldn't have done better. I was relieved when the horses were back in their pasture, but I had seen another glimpse of my cowboy.

On the way home, Hyrum told me about his military training on M-14 guns and his "expert" marksmanship pin. Knowing of my gun collection, he suggested that we get a rifle and go shooting. Stopping at the house long enough to get my bolt-action .22, we drove to the old dump on the north side of St. George. While Hyrum loaded the gun, I found a couple of empty whiskey bottles and placed them on the hood of a rusted car, some 100 feet away.

When I returned, he handed me the gun and said, "You shoot first."

"Which part of the bottle would you like me to hit?"

Thinking I was joking, he laughed, "Aw, why don't you start at the top?"

As I carefully aimed, the picture of his marksmanship pin came into my mind. *I'd better shoot straight,* I thought, then fired three shots: taking first the cap, then the neck, and then the base of the bottle. He surprised me with his compliment. "Gail, that's wonderful! I wish I could shoot like that." (I didn't know at the time that he had earned his pin by shooting 100 rounds of ammunition from an M-60 machine gun into a large target on the hillside.) After we had emptied a box of .22 bullets, he asked, "How about a game of tennis?"

A flashback of earlier tennis dates automatically kicked in the old familiar mental process: *Should I let him win?* Then I realized I was with Hyrum. There was no need. I laughed and asked, "If I win, will you still give me a ride home?" I did, and he did.

After such a long, active day, we had earned our supper. Later that night, Hyrum asked me to come with him to the St. George Temple. Because of the late hour the gates to the grounds were closed, so we had to step over the three-foot, wrought-iron fence to get in. As we strolled along the walk, arm in arm, admiring the brilliantly lit temple and smelling the fresh spring air, Hyrum asked me if I had ever been to Washington, D.C., and visited our nation's capitol. My answer was no.

He then asked, "How is your imagination?" Before I could answer, he told me that when he found the right spot, he was going to tell me a story that would require an imagination.

We approached the front of the temple with its two massive staircases leading up to the enormous front doors. At the sides of the staircases the gardeners had readied the ground for the spring planting of flowers. Hyrum took me by the hand and led me to the right staircase. Beaming, he declared, "This is the right spot."

Kneeling down on the freshly cultivated soil, he smoothed out a section of dirt with his hand and began drawing a map with his index finger. I was leaning over his shoulder, trying to imagine what he was about to show me. Finally, after completing his drawings, he began to explain: "Imagine you are in Washington, D.C." Marking each place, he showed me where the Lincoln Memorial was in relationship to the Jefferson Memorial, the Potomac River, the Washington Monument, and the Capitol. Hyrum then asked me to step up on the staircase to about the fourth stair. He remained at the base of the stairs looking up at me.

"Now imagine that you are standing on the steps of the Lincoln Memorial looking toward the Washington Monument," he said. "Looking over your shoulder is Abraham Lincoln sitting in his enormous chair. He is looking at the same picture. In front of you is a beautiful rectangular reflection pool that extends almost to the Washington Monument. The reflection of the monument in the pool comes back and almost touches you. Beyond the Washington Monument on the hill is America's beautifully lit Capitol. Can you imagine the picture, Gail?"

"I not only see it, I can feel it!" I answered.

He continued, "Three years ago, a dear friend of mine, Arty Gaines, and I stood on those very stairs and basked in that scene. We were touched by the spirit of the great patriots. We made a pact between us that when each of us met the girl he would marry, he would ask for her hand in marriage on the steps of the Lincoln Memorial. Since it is physically impossible for us to be there, you will have to imagine it. Gail, will you marry me?"

The Hitching Post

Some situations have to be handled delicately and artfully. I didn't worry about my mother, but I did hesitate to tell Dad about our wedding plans, for several reasons. I knew my dad had looked forward to the return of his gardening and cowboy sidekick. Traditions run deep, and I knew he looked on Hyrum as a foreigner to our folksy, small-town culture. Hyrum possessed little of the farmer brawn and background; therefore, he was likely to whisk me away from my Dixie roots to a faraway city in order to make a living. My dad had always resisted change, and deciding to get married after three days of formal courting was instant change. Dad needed time. Hyrum planned to return in two weeks. Meanwhile, I could prepare the soil for the big seed.

When Hyrum returned from Fort Ord to officially ask my father for my hand, we decided to get what was on our minds *off* our minds right away. I asked my parents to come into the living room and sit on the piano bench, then timidly shifted responsibility to Hyrum: "Hyrum needs to talk to you." After a few minutes of nervous small talk, Hyrum asked the big question. "I'm in love with your daughter. May I have her hand in marriage?"

The reaction every young girl anticipates and wants from her parents came instantly and intuitively from my mother, who exclaimed, "Oh, this is wonderful!" The response most dreaded came from my father; even I wasn't prepared for his stern and stiff reaction. He coldly asked Hyrum how he planned to support me and where we planned to live. Hyrum didn't have a good answer for either question. Without a word, Dad stood up and walked out of the room.

That was when Hyrum decided to apply for Officer's Candidate School. He knew that a private's pay couldn't meet Dad's expectations—or our needs. Besides, with the military buildup occurring at the time in Vietnam, he decided he would rather serve his time as an officer than as an enlisted man. The OCS training would also buy six more months on American soil.

Over the next few months, while we waited for Hyrum's accep-
tance into OCS, we did our courting on weekend passes or
extended leaves from Fort Ord. On one such weekend, we had
decided to meet at Mother Ruth's temporary home in Provo. (At
age sixty-three, she was working on her master's degree at Brigham
Young University.) Hyrum had driven all night for this rendezvous,
so Hyrum's mother, his sister Pauline, and I were relieved to see his
car pull safely into the driveway. We rushed outside to meet him.
As Hyrum approached his welcoming committee, I held back out
of respect for Mother Ruth, assuming that he would want to greet
her first. To my surprise and pleasure, he boldly strode past his
mother and sister to gather me into his arms and kiss me. "I drove
all night to see *you*," he whispered in my ear. That simple expression was pivotal; it reinforced that I was number one in his life.

In June, his orders arrived: Hyrum was to report to Fort Sill,
Oklahoma, on July 1. Before his transfer, we were able to spend ten
days together, in which time we did six months' worth of planning.
First on Hyrum's agenda was to surprise me with a beautiful silver
and diamond engagement ring. He also felt it important that we
begin paying on a car so that we would have our own when we
married. He had saved about $600 for the down payment; with his
mother as a cosigner, we financed a new $2,500 1966 Rambler
Classic. My mother later named our new acquisition "the surrey
with the red fringe on top," because it was white with a red top.
Next on the agenda was to make our wedding plans. We decided
that we would be married in the St. George Temple on December
twenty-first, right after his graduation on the seventeenth. As a
parting gift, Hyrum presented me with a bandolier filled with
twenty-four spent machine-gun cartridges, instructing me that each
Sunday night, after his telephone call, I was to pull out one shell to
represent the passing of another week.

It was a wonderful Dixieland summer. Early each morning,
before the sun could speak its heated language, I found myself
beside Dad landscaping the backyard of the rest home. It didn't take

long for my England-blanched face and arms to tan and my hands to regain their calluses. It was a summer of nostalgia: I was working alongside my dad as in times of yore. When the blazing sun cast no shadow, we sought the grumble of the swamp cooler churning to cool the house. Evenings would find Mom, Dad, and me on the river bottom in Washington, riding horses and doing the chores. Sometimes we would finish the chores early, pack a watermelon, and drive to Pine Valley to cool off and fish. I savored each moment because I knew that such a summer as this one with my parents would not come again. From now on I would be with Hyrum; we had at least two more years to spend in the army, a university degree to obtain, employment to find, and settling into a home to do. The spent cartridges in the machine-gun bandolier emptied faster than I could have imagined.

I remember the last Sunday of November, when Hyrum called to announce that he would be the honor graduate of his OCS class and to tell me that, as his fiancée, I would be expected to pin on the gold bars indicating his rank as second lieutenant. I would have a personal escort for the proceedings and Hyrum and I would be expected to lead off the dancing at the grand military ball. This phone call caused me great anxiety. Never in my wildest dreams had I ever imagined that this small-town girl would be involved in such elaborate proceedings. I was completely unfamiliar with military protocol and even unsure about what I should wear. I felt like Eliza Doolittle of *My Fair Lady* fame; however, I was not so sure that I could bring off the necessary transformation.

A month earlier, Hyrum's brother, Denis, who had recently returned from serving in Vietnam, had brought me some beautiful Vietnamese material—deep aqua silk, brocaded with fine gold thread—with the idea that I might use it to make a formal gown. I persuaded my friend Delores, a talented seamstress, to transform this material into a dress befitting a military ball. Then, once again, Mom and I searched madly all over St. George for the perfect shoes to match my dress. Mother Ruth gave me some long, white, pearl-buttoned gloves to wear with the gown. Throughout all these preparations, my dad kept teasing me with statements like, "Nose in the air and walk with poise, Mademoiselle," or "May I seat you, Your Highness?" His joking didn't make me any more comfortable with the image I had of the glamorous ball in which I was expected to be the leading lady.

The day of the big event finally arrived. The promised escort, Lieutenant Retzlaff, met our plane in Oklahoma and immediately whisked us off to the Pass in Review parade. The grandstands bulged with proud supporters of the graduating officers and thousands of future candidates. It was easy to get caught up in the charismatic, powerful atmosphere: flags waving, bands playing patriotic music, and 3,600 sharply dressed American soldiers marching in formation. I didn't need binoculars to focus on my handsome honor graduate as he led his battalion past.

After the march music halted, the grandstand crowd swept into the auditorium for the graduation and awards ceremonies. Lieutenant Retzlaff escorted me to the front row with the wives of the high-ranking military officers. After a rousing military Pledge of Allegiance, the school commandant called Hyrum to the stand and boasted that of all the OCS graduates who had passed through this school, Hyrum's composite scores ranked the highest. The colonel then signaled Lieutenant Retzlaff to escort me to the stand to fasten Hyrum's second-lieutenant bars on his left shoulder while he pinned the bars on Hyrum's right shoulder.

Shaking with stage fright, I took the gold bars from their small box and stretched up on my toes to better see the shoulder flap. Struggling to appear dainty as I tried to force the gold posts through the thick material, I placed my thumb under the flap to avoid sticking the posts into Hyrum's shoulder. With a burst of adrenaline, I forced the pin straight through the material and deep into my thumb. A bright red stream of blood shot from the puncture wound. Silently wincing in pain, I carefully pushed the other post through the material and snapped the two fasteners into place, praying that no one in the audience would notice the stains on the gold bar. Despite the bloody throbbing in my thumb, pain did not dampen my pride as I heard the words: "Hyrum Wayne Smith, I commission you a second lieutenant in the United States Army."

The excitement of the parade and graduation melted in my anticipation for the grand ball. I gazed into the mirror that reflected my transformation, feeling foreign and far from home in the aqua gown and long gloves. My simple, rural upbringing had not readied me for such an occasion, yet I sensed that this new image in the mirror reflected a glimpse of my future. The knock on the door reminded me of the time. I took a last wistful glance, then opened the door to my second lieutenant in his Class A uniform. Hyrum's gold bars, now shiny, glistened in the light.

The enormous ballroom, romantically lit, was magnificent. A sparkling mirrored ball hung from the ceiling, casting millions of brilliant reflections off the glittering jewelry, elegant formal dresses, and bright gold officers' bars. As the orchestra played the enchanting strains of our love song, "More," it was our cue to begin the dance. Hyrum held me close and softly sang the lyrics, "Longer than always is a long, long time; but far beyond forever you'll be mine." The words of the song and the feeling of his strong arms securely around me brought eternity into perspective. The fading shadows of my past connected comfortably with the not-so-frightening unknowns of the future. Five days later, on December 21, 1966, Hyrum and I began our eternal journey together.

7

A bird and a song

To Hyrum and me, planning and preparing for a family was the pinnacle of commitment and responsibility in our marriage. Children are a joyous investment that begins at conception and extends into the eternities. The risks of pregnancy are brought acutely into focus by the pain of birthing and all the complications that can arise during those critical minutes. But that's just the beginning. The moment of birth initiates the lifelong need for nourishing, protecting, teaching, providing, caring, and loving.

Outside forces are often overwhelming and always pressing in on a family in one form or another: finances, illnesses, education, accidents, even death. But with faith in God's eternal plan and in his purposes for his spirit children, Hyrum and I began our family.

Six Children, Six Treasures

After we had been married about four months, Hyrum was stationed in Germany. We moved to a quaint village, Oberberinglin, about eight miles from the U.S. military base at Schwäbisch Gmünd in West Germany. There we were, newlyweds in a foreign land, unable to speak German and unfamiliar with the military lifestyle and protocol. Though the scenes through my window were reminiscent of the landscapes of my small farming town, I was very aware of the miles of ocean separating me from my roots. Just a few months into this adventure, we discovered that I was pregnant. We were thrilled, but the news further increased my awareness of the distance from home. Suddenly, living in Germany seemed less like an adventure and more like a peril to be feared.

I wrote the news home to my family and begged my mother to come be with me in April—the baby was due the twenty-fifth. Dad, bless his generous heart, was willing to sell a couple of cows to finance the trip for my mother and my sister Nola. Knowing they were coming, I felt much less alone.

I felt all right during the pregnancy, but examinations at the prenatal clinic were invariably traumatic. I was always reminded of running cows through the squeeze chute for branding, shots, and pregnancy tests. Visiting the doctor for prenatal care at a military health-care facility involved being herded into one of ten rooms on two sides of a hallway, never seeing the same doctor twice. Being a newcomer to childbearing, I wasn't sure whether my twinges and symptoms were normal or ominous. That uncertainty raised my anxiety level even higher than that created by the impersonal, cattle-herd environment. Add to that the fact that Hyrum had to be gone thirty days out of ninety, and the stress of that first pregnancy becomes easy to imagine.

Hyrum and I busied ourselves preparing a nursery, buying diapers and pins and bottles and bibs, and fantasizing about what it would be like to have our own little boy or girl. We wondered if we should buy blue or pink and ended up with a lot of yellow. Choosing names was easy: If we had a boy, we would name him after the grandfathers, Joseph Evan. A girl would be named Glenna Ruth, after her grandmothers. Our preparations consumed the nine months quickly.

When we picked up my mother and sister at the airport, Mom's very presence assured me that everything would be all right. As we drove to Oberberinglin, an hour and a half away, I explained that I had a doctor's appointment scheduled for the next morning; they could catch up on their much-needed sleep while Hyrum accompanied me. Little did I know that the backache I was experiencing even as I spoke to Mom meant I wouldn't actually see her again until three days later, when I arrived home with our eight-pound, three-ounce daughter, Glenna.

The breech delivery was long and exhausting. This was before fathers were encouraged to be labor coaches, so Hyrum was not with me. Instead, a doctor and three nurses were talking to me, coaching me, and pushing on my abdomen. I remember being so exhausted I could feel myself lose consciousness between contractions, totally spent. I heard the nurse insist, "One more time, Gail. You've got to."

I pled with my Heavenly Father to give me the energy to try one more time. I had never felt so depleted, never experienced such excruciating pain. But I tried once more, and finally they were able to get hold of Glenna's slick little bottom and help her be delivered. I barely realized that she was born, except that the pain stopped. I was totally exhausted. When they let Hyrum in to see me and the baby, he almost went into shock at the sight of all the blood. It was a very scary time for both of us.

Hyrum had a special present for me—a .22 Ruger pistol with wood handle in a holster. Not every woman would treasure such a gift, I know, but it was just right for me with my love for guns.

The three weeks that Mom stayed passed like a flash of lightning. During that time, she taught me how to wash the diapers and fold them into perfect triangles, how to mix just the right amount of formula at just the right temperature, how to test the bath water with my elbow or wrist to be sure it wasn't too cold or too hot, how to lay out the towel, washcloth, soap, and clean clothes in order so they would be handy but in no danger of being splashed, and how to keep soap out of the baby's eyes while washing her hair, her back, and her tummy. "And be careful of the soft spot," she would remind me. Mom took pride in showing me how to carefully wrap our "earth angel" in the blankets and how to hold her with confidence. (I still wasn't sure that she wouldn't break.) By the end of three weeks, thanks to Mom, I had a system for dealing with the physical needs of our new arrival.

Mom arose early on her last day to wash and fold the diapers, then help me bathe, dress, and feed her little namesake one last time before we took her and Nola back to the Stuttgart Airport. As we got closer and closer, the lump in my throat got bigger and bigger. After they boarded the plane, Hyrum and I stood close together, holding the precious bundle that Mom had so expertly wrapped and watching their departure through the large-paned window. We walked back to the car in silence. I couldn't speak; tears were too close to the surface. Mom had taught me well, but who would reassure me when uncertainty set in?

As the three of us settled into the car, the full impact of our own family journey came into focus. This beautiful, helpless blessing needed our unconditional love, care, and guidance. We, her parents, would be the most influential force in her life. We needed to keep growing up ourselves, besides providing for this precious child opportunities for progression like those our parents had given us.

I shed a few tears, but at least I could talk. Hyrum and I reviewed our plan to teach and transplant those values we wanted our children to have. We had talked about them before, even before we married, and many times after we learned I was pregnant. But now we discussed our family goals intensely, soberly, as if we were making a kind of promise to little Glenna and to God.

First, because spiritual values had been so influential in our own lives, we wanted Glenna to have experiences that would help her know and appreciate God. Accordingly, we committed to each other that we would have daily personal and family prayer. We would read the scriptures daily as a family. We would try to do willingly everything God required of us, to serve and love others and to fulfill our church commitments.

Second, having a close and loving family was important to us, so we decided that we would hold regular family home evenings, setting aside that weekly time to learn and play together. We would establish strong family traditions that would pull the family together even after the children were grown and on their own. We

determined that every year we would take a family vacation, work-ing together to earn the necessary money to visit other places and meet new people and cultures.

Third, to build our children's self-esteem and confidence, we would involve them at an early age in athletics, music, and other activities that would allow them to discover and develop their tal-ents.

Fourth, we would establish a budget that would allow us to remain debt free. The only things we would buy on time would be a house and vehicles, and the children would learn how to man-age their personal finances.

Fifth, we would help our children learn the value of work and the discipline that comes with good work habits.

To help us keep our commitment to successfully transplant those values, we decided that we would establish annual personal and family goals and review them as the year progressed. It wouldn't be easy; but we knew that if it were left to chance or to others, the transfer would probably not happen. We felt solemn, our hearts bursting with love and a passionate desire to do our best for this precious little person, the first of what we hoped would be many children. From that love would come the discipline and con-sistency we knew we would need in accomplishing all these things. We also knew that the example we set in pursuing our values would help create the kind of family environment needed for our children to succeed on their own.

By the time we got home, it was Glenna's feeding time. We walked into the kitchen and, out of habit, opened the refrigerator to retrieve a bottle. Seven bottles of formula, prepared by my mother as a last loving gesture, were neatly lined up in the refriger-ator door. I hugged Glenna tightly and began to weep. Sensing my feelings, Hyrum put his arms tenderly around both of us. Taped to one of the bottles was Mom's note expressing her love for Hyrum, me, and her namesake. Mom knew. She had provided for our needs one more day.

How quickly things can change! Glenna was born in April 1968, and by December of that year Hyrum had completed his military service and we were on our way home. After spending Christmas with Hyrum's family in Hawaii, we moved to Provo, Utah, where we soon settled in as struggling students at Brigham Young University. And I found myself pregnant once again.

Following eighteen months on the heels of Glenna, this new arrival would, I hoped, be born on my mother's birthday, November 10. Two days earlier than the hoped-for time, Stacie Gail entered mortality at Provo's Utah Valley Hospital, weighing in at a respectable seven pounds, fourteen ounces. I had considered naming her Jerusha Gail, after the first wife of a much earlier Hyrum Smith in the family ancestral line. But I was apparently the only one who liked that name, and family pressures prevailed—we named her Stacie Gail Smith. She was quickly nicknamed "Little Ace."

All too soon following Stacie's arrival, I was surprised to find myself pregnant once more. As a family of four, with two babies only eighteen months apart, we were just barely stretching our monthly G.I. Bill payments of $250 far enough. How could we pay for a third child? Hyrum was pouring his energies into his studies and his spare time into a revitalized troop of seventeen Explorer Scouts who had been working their hearts out since September to raise enough money for a dream trip to Hawaii the next summer. He needed my help and support.

Fortunately, I hadn't had difficult pregnancies up to that point, so both Hyrum and I decided not to tell anyone about this one until after the Hawaii trip was over, when I would be six months pregnant. With judiciously baggy clothes and two little daughters as camouflage, we would be all right. And we were—the experience in Hawaii was a high point in our lives.

On November 25, 1970, little more than a year after Stacie's birth and again in Utah Valley Hospital, I gave birth to a girl with a thick mop of black hair that hung down her neck. In fact, after she was born I shared a hospital room with a Navajo woman who had just given birth to a beautiful baby boy. On one occasion the nurse brought the babies in and, without checking their identification, gave my dark-haired Sharwan to the Indian mother and her baby to me. Since that day, I have always thought of my "Wannie" as my "Indian princess."

Sharwan's conception was a surprise, but we planned and prayed for Joseph. Things were not on quite as short a fuse with him—Joseph arrived more than two and a half years after Sharwan. In the interim, Hyrum had graduated from Brigham Young University, and after a brief time during which he sold insurance in Hawaii, we moved to Portland, Oregon, where Hyrum had accepted a position with a growing computer services firm.

At the point when my pregnancy was confirmed, Hyrum, who identified strongly with his male ancestors, was convinced that this child would be a son. As the pregnancy advanced, he chatted happily about "our son" and dated things by "when my boy is born." His absolute assurance went past being funny for some ward members, and one woman, the Relief Society president, became so frustrated and anxious that she simply let him have it one day. "Bishop Smith," she scolded, "you just cannot put that pressure on your wife. It's not fair." Hyrum just laughed, and we and the entire ward waited to see if his assurances were indeed prophetic.

Joseph Evan, named after his grandfathers, was not only our first boy and also the first baby to arrive normally (head first), but he was huge—ten and one-half pounds. He was big all over, with big hands and big feet. The nurse attending his delivery exclaimed, "Great Scott! He has the shoulders of a football player!"

Hyrum was elated. When I got home from the hospital a few days later, a huge banner adorned the garage: "It's a boy!" The Relief Society president and other members of the ward breathed a sigh of relief.

After Joe's birth in June of 1973, I was surprised to discover in November or early December that I was expecting again. It was really too soon after having Joseph, who had been such a big baby.

I hadn't had time to recover, and my body was protesting. (My difficulties during this pregnancy are part of another story, to be told
in more detail below.) We were all relieved and very happy when
our fifth child was born on July 16, 1974. We named her Rebecca
Devan, her middle name rhyming with my father's name, Evan.

Because Rebecca's birth created some medical problems for me,
our doctor urgently recommended that I have no more children.
We accepted his recommendation, even though we had a strong
feeling that our family was not complete. Joseph needed a little
brother to balance things out somewhat. We realized that, in some
ways, he was pretty outnumbered as the only boy with four sisters.

We applied to adopt another boy through LDS Social Services,
but the social worker held out no hope. "Babies are for those who
have no children, and you've got five," he pointed out. He appraised
our chances at "a million to impossible" and asked if we would
consider adopting an older child, possibly one with a handicap. We
agreed, and the process began: a social worker inspected our home,
interviewed us, checked on our family life, and monitored us. We
moved to California in the middle of the process and asked that the
adoption service be transferred, only to learn that we had to start
the process all over again. Again we submitted to their require-
ments. Again, they discouraged us about the possibility of ever
finding a child.

Unbeknownst to us, Jacob was born in May 1976 when
Rebecca was almost two—just the time we probably would have
had a child of our own, if that had been possible. His first four
years were spent in trying circumstances; his mother, unable to
cope with the demands of her life, sometimes abused and neglected
him.

In June 1980, we received a wonderful call: "You'll never believe
this, but we have a four-year-old boy who we feel belongs in your
family. Are you still interested?"

That night we held a special family home evening. We

discussed the pros and cons of adding a four-year-old to our family (almost no one could think of any cons), fixed up a bed in Joseph's room (he was very proud to be a big brother), then drove together to the agency where we met Jacob. It was love at first sight. He had bright blond hair. His face was radiant with laughter. I could tell he was a fun-loving boy. As we got back in the van, I kept him on my lap with my arms around him. He settled back against me, his little shoulders just relaxing like a sigh of relief. It seemed to be both physical and mental relief on his part.

Our other children were just leaving to spend a month in Utah with their grandparents, but Hyrum and I kept Jacob with us so that we could concentrate on him as the "honeymoon" wore off. It was a smooth transition, a great foundation for the loving and stable relationship that began to form. We never had the slightest doubt that Jacob was meant for our family, even though his birth mother had a year in which to change her mind about the adoption. When a combination of financial and emotional problems had forced Jacob's mother to give him up for adoption, she had told the agency that she wanted him to go into a good home with a loving and close family that practiced Mormon values. When she did the required evaluation at the end of the trial period of the adoption, she watched Jacob play with Joseph and Becca through the one-way glass at the agency office. The social worker later told us that she said, "He doesn't wear a plastic smile anymore. It's okay. I know he's happy and being taken care of." She signed the final papers.

Our "Jaker" has brought us the same joys and frustrations and memories as all our children. His coming to our family was an answer to prayer. We are all grateful for him.

Those are our six children, our six treasures. I think we would have had a dozen, if we could have. Each child brings a great joy into our family. Our desire to teach these unique individuals well and to give them confidence, competence, and compassion shaped our lives from the moment they arrived.

A Learning Time

Our family's systematic plan for teaching our children important skills, values, and attitudes emerged from my difficult fifth pregnancy. Because of medical complications, the doctor gave me three choices: have an abortion, maintain normal activity and miscarry, or stay in bed. For us, the decision was an easy one: Even though there were no guarantees that the pregnancy would proceed normally to term anyway, I went to bed.

This forced inactivity was difficult for me in many ways. I had always been so strong, so capable physically. I couldn't understand. Why me? Why now? I had thought of myself as the one with the strength and will to help others through life's struggles. It was hard to see myself in this new way.

And it was hard, as well, not to *do*. Any mother with four children ages five and under knows how needed a mother's hands, voice, and eyes are. Could I still tend to the tasks of mothering while this aspect of maternity immobilized me? Hyrum would help me all he could, but he was gone a lot because of his work. When he was home, many of his evening and weekend hours went to serving in the stake presidency. Kind neighbors and friends willingly did my grocery shopping and heavy housecleaning; they often brought in dinner for us, and we could not have managed without their kindness.

Despite our apprehensions, Hyrum and I saw this family crisis as a family opportunity. We talked seriously with our daughters. Glenna would turn six in three months. Stacie was four, Sharwan three, and little Joseph was five months old as this strange season in our lives began. We explained our dilemma in terms they could understand, and asked if they would help. Without realizing the seriousness of the medical situation, they unhesitatingly threw themselves into the role of "Mama's helpers," going far beyond what we expected at first they would be capable of.

Here was our routine. Each morning around 6:30 A.M. the girls rose, dressed themselves, made their own beds, straightened their rooms, and started a load of Joseph's diapers in the wash. The little wooden stools that Grandma Smith had made by hand and painted for each child the Christmas before became permanent fixtures in front of the washing machine and kitchen stove.

The breakfast menu was simple: French toast, oatmeal, or prepared cereal. I could get up long enough to walk to the kitchen table to eat with them and to feed Joseph. (Glenna and Stacie would put him in his infant seat or high chair for me.) I can still picture the girls, chemist-like, carefully pouring the already prepared formula to the right line on the bottle.

After breakfast the older girls rinsed the dishes and placed them in the dishwasher. Three-year-old Sharwan monopolized the job of turning the dial to start the dishwasher.

Next, the girls would return to the laundry room. Glenna, standing on her green stool, would pull Joseph's freshly washed diapers out of the washing machine and hand them to four-year-old Stacie to put in the dryer. Glenna was just tall enough to twist the dials to turn on the dryer. Carefully sorting the rest of the accumulated laundry into towels, lights, and darks, they would start the next batch of laundry. Fortunately, we were in the perma-press era. If we removed Hyrum's shirts from the dryer quickly, we didn't have to worry about wrinkles.

When Joseph's diapers came out, all three girls would sit on the living-room floor, stacking and smoothing the squares of bird's-eye muslin. Then, as I had taught them, they laboriously folded each one into a kite shape for their brother and stacked them on the shelves of his little changing table.

Another major job was changing Joseph's diapers. Of necessity, the girls learned how. Granted, the diapers weren't always perfectly positioned, but the plastic pants helped to secure them. If it looked like a big job, Glenna and Stacie would wrap their arms around Joseph's middle and lug all twenty pounds of him in to me.

Lunch was a thickly spread peanut butter and honey sandwich or a bowl of canned soup and a glass of milk. As for dinners,

Hyrum arranged to stay in town as often as possible; when he *was* around, his cooking consisted mainly of Kentucky Fried Chicken or hamburgers from McDonald's or the newly arrived Burger King. Thankfully, my mother was able to come visit, a week at a time, on two separate occasions, and Hyrum's mother also stayed with us twice. Their efforts, combined with those of the dear neighbors and ward members who often brought in meals, helped us survive the experience.

My bed became the game table, reading room, and schoolhouse. Glenna learned to read, months before she started kindergarten, from Dr. Seuss's *Hop on Pop*. Our favorite card games were Fish, Concentration, and King's Corner. We put together puzzles, read fairy tales, Bible stories, and children's books, and sang hundreds of songs, from Grandpa Cooper's "Wise Old Spider" to the ever-popular "ABC" song.

I watched Joseph as his sisters coached him in sitting up, crawling, climbing, and standing. As his first birthday approached in June, they taught him to walk, one holding him at one end of the room while another coaxed him toward her outstretched arms. Indelible in my mind is an image of Joe in brown shorts and a brown-checked shirt, his face split by an enormous grin as he toddled triumphantly back and forth.

Hyrum and I marveled at the joyful competence our daughters developed. Anything within the limits of their physical strength that we could describe, explain, or demonstrate, they could do. This confirmed my feeling that achievement is a direct result of expectations. I expressed gratitude and appreciation often to them. My little children were rising—rising to the occasion, rising up in triumph—and my heart swelled with joy. I honestly think that through their simple, childlike faith, they knew how important their service was for this unborn child. They could feel that they were a necessary part of something eternal. I think it was a natural response for them to excitedly exclaim: "We can do it, Mama!" It seemed that my children expected a great deal of themselves, and they recognized that they could rise to meet those expectations.

I am convinced that we should not sell our children short nor trivialize their ability to learn on their personal timetables. We need to be thoughtful about potential opportunities, skeptical about conventional wisdom, and discerning about when the time is right for each particular child.

Even though mothering from bed was as challenging and time-consuming as anything I had ever done, I spent a lot of time thinking. Although I would never have willingly chosen to spend six months in bed, my children were naturally learning the values of hard work and cooperation that I had learned as a child on the family farm. They really were doing just fine. Aside from a box of cornflakes left on the stove that caught on fire when Glenna turned on the burner, we had relatively few mishaps.

Yes, the children were doing a great job, but what would happen after the birth? Their efficient system of homemaking, their easy communication and negotiation with each other over the tasks and how to do them, would almost certainly be disrupted when I took up the usual roles as mother and homemaker. How could I continue this wonderful learning curve without spending more time in bed?

The challenge, as I saw it, was that we had no cows to milk, no hay to haul, and no fires to build. But we did have a house, yard, garden, dishes, laundry, bedrooms, and piano. We could involve the children in goal planning, scripture reading, athletics, education, and family projects. Somehow we could construct a system similar to the one the children were using in this "emergency," a system that could become part of our daily routine and help accomplish the goals that Hyrum and I had set for our family.

When Rebecca was born, six weeks premature but completely healthy, I was very excited about her birth, about my new mobility, and about trying out my ideas.

A thousand songs

I believe that a house is the shelter you wrap around a home. Not all houses are homes. Not all homes are made in houses. It is the bond among family members that creates a home. Still, I believe strongly in the power of place to shape our responses and to give us a safe yet stimulating environment for learning. When place and people come together, special things can happen.

I think the term *homemaker* is a thrilling one, packed with power and promise. Although our society applies it usually to women and often uses it as a synonym for *housewife*, *homemaker* is a title that applies to everyone—husband, wife, children, grandparents, aunts, uncles, cousins, even the family dog—who cares about and works for the quality of life within the home.

Part of the reason Hyrum and I teach our children to do housework in the way that we do is because we don't have a farm or a workshop, as many families had in past times. Our home is the arena where we teach the principles of work. But there's another reason. We want them to be not only housekeepers, but also homemakers—sons and daughters alike.

As our children grew and began school, their individual talents began to emerge. We felt an increasing need to coordinate the many personal, business, school, and church activities we were all involved with. As our needs evolved, our system gradually took on a fuller shape. Then, in the fall of 1977, we received an enormous opportunity—a calling to preside over the California Ventura Mission for three years.

The years that we served in the mission field further contributed to the development of our family training ideas. Missionary rules had not changed since Hyrum and I had served in England. The only difference was that now, as leaders, we set the pace. Just as the missionaries were expected to arise at 6:00 A.M., pray, read the scriptures, and prepare for the day, so did the Smiths—all of them. The children were on this mission just as much as we were, and they prided themselves on their obedience to the mission rules.

While we were in California, the children became very involved in the community athletics programs. And we were fortunate to find a wonderful, dedicated piano teacher, Connie Tice, who was firm but loving, had high expectations for her students, and gave them many opportunities to perform. She laid a solid foundation for the budding musical careers of my children. The mission calling itself provided many other opportunities, such as fulfilling speaking assignments or singing together at conferences and church functions.

After our mission, we relocated to Centerville, Utah, a pleasant, semirural community thirteen miles north of Salt Lake City. When we moved into our Centerville home, it was easy to transfer the mission routine into our "normal" life. Glenna was fourteen and going into ninth grade, with the other children stair-stepping down in age to six-year-old Jacob, just entering first grade. In the mission field, we had kept our schedules in simple pocket calendars. Now, as we maintained and integrated our mission-inspired morning schedule into the daily routine of our household in Centerville, we were very grateful for the more advanced day planner and time management system that Hyrum was now teaching in seminars.

As the children grew older, their schedules became more complex (as did mine and Hyrum's). If Hyrum's work hadn't introduced day planners into our lives, I would have had to invent one just to keep straight the after-school schedule of carpooling to practices, games, and lessons. Besides the boiling activity brought on by community, school, and church events, I still had a household to maintain—thus, the compelling need for the full incorporation of the Magic Three Hours.

The Magic Three Hours

Fourteen years earlier, during the ride home from the Stuttgart airport with our three-week-old baby, Hyrum and I had defined our desires for our children. As we thought back to that important time of commitment to our baby and our other future children, we were desirous to fully implement that commitment. We wanted our children to be confident, competent, and compassionate—anywhere in the world. They had to possess real skills. They had to be self-sufficient and have self-esteem. The compassion needed to come from three sources: deep religious roots that connected them in a personal way with a loving Heavenly Father; the example in our family life of recognizing, honoring, and meeting each other's needs; and the practice of serving others cheerfully, willingly, and spontaneously. We had committed ourselves to those values then, and had already done much to implement that commitment. But now, the seeds that had been planted fourteen years earlier were about to begin their full flowering.

"The Magic Three Hours" was the name we gave the plan that systematized and expanded on the methods we were already using to teach our children. It gave us a way of building important events into the schedule, instead of hoping somehow we could make time for them. It didn't take us long to figure out when to hold our magic hours—they obviously had to be during a time when no one else wanted us or our children. Afternoons were always crowded with friends, homework, athletics, music lessons, telephone calls, the unexpected events that regularly surface—and fatigue. The magic, uninterrupted hours would have to occur in the early morning.

Each morning, Hyrum and I would wake up fifteen minutes before the kick-off moment, pray, dress for exercising, and then move systematically through the house, waking each child individually, helping him or her make the bed, then kneeling together for the child's individual prayers. This was always the sweetest experience of the day for me, as I listened to my children express through prayer their gratitude, their concerns, their simple needs, and their inner desires. Their pure, unpretentious communication with God continually reminded me of my children's unquestioning faith and of my eternal responsibility to them as their mother.

The hour for beginning the Magic Three Hours has varied from year to year, defined by the time our children had to leave for school and the various jobs they had to accomplish within our magic hours. In the beginning, when all the children were in elementary school, which started at 9:00 A.M., rising at 6:30 A.M. worked fine. But high school started at 7:30 A.M., so as a family we discussed what we should do. The children decided to move the getting–up hour to 5:00 A.M. It was exciting for Hyrum and me to see the children make this choice, because we realized that they had internalized the power of the Magic Three Hours. They recognized for themselves that this was the most effective way to accomplish our personal and family goals.

When everyone was up (notice I don't use the word *awake*), we all gathered in the study at the "round table," a circular table that seated all eight of us. First we planned our day and reviewed our schedules so that when the chauffeur's hat went on my head I would know where and when to pick up each of the children. Next we would read and discuss a chapter from the book of scripture we had chosen to study that year. Then we knelt as a family and Hyrum would call on one of us to offer the family prayer.

From here we would break off into our various morning assignments. The children practiced the piano (by 1983 we had two pianos to accommodate six practice sessions in a three-hour period), started the laundry, emptied the dishwasher, made breakfast, fixed school lunches, set the table, tidied up the bathrooms, and finalized school preparations. Hyrum and I supervised, exercised, made dinner preparations, or otherwise got ready for the day. The breakfast call came at 7:00 A.M. After breakfast, some children had clean-up duty, some finished with piano practice, and some had to leave for school.

By the time the last child left for school, the house was in order: the beds were made, the bathrooms were cleaned, the laundry was done, dishes were washed, and dinner was ready to put in the oven at the appropriate time. Rather than facing a day of endless housework, I could meet my own busy schedule, have some time for myself, and be fully available to the children and to Hyrum after school and in the evenings.

Afternoons brought household chores, athletic games and practices, music lessons, homework, dinner, an hour for bedtime preparations, and an early bedtime—8:00 P.M. Eating dinner together was an important priority for us. Though I didn't really learn to cook until after I was married (with the Betty Crocker step-by-step *Cooking for Two* as my guide) and have never claimed to be an expert chef, I can put together the basic food groups tastefully and make a mean pot of chili. Our meals were tasty, nutritious, and simple. More important than a fancy meal was the time we spent together at the table. I believe that eating together is a strengthening time, a bonding time, a healing time. Hyrum and the kids came in from the daily "battle" at school or work to the safety and reassurance of family. The mealtime was the time to reflect upon the day's events; for us as parents, it was always a listening time and sometimes a teaching time. It was a time for prayer and thanksgiving. A hot, delicious meal was soothing and pleasurable, a daily reward we all looked forward to. There were obviously instances when eating together was impossible, but we made it a high priority and achieved it a surprising number of times.

A sample of one day's schedule from 1986 tells the story in a nutshell. Glenna was a senior in high school, Stacie a junior, Sharwan a sophomore; Joe was an eighth grader, Becca a seventh grader, and Jacob a fifth grader. This was how a typical day went:

5:00 A.M.　Arise, make beds, dress

5:10 A.M.　Read scriptures

5:30 A.M.　Glenna and Stacie—piano
　　　　　　Sharwan—laundry/school preparations
　　　　　　Joseph, Rebecca, Jacob—pre-breakfast (empty
　　　　　　dishwasher, set table, cook breakfast, make
　　　　　　school lunches)

6:00 A.M.　Sharwan—piano
　　　　　　Stacie—tidy bathrooms/school preparations

6:45 A.M.　Breakfast—family
　　　　　　Final school preparation

7:15 A.M.　High schoolers leave
　　　　　　Joseph and Rebecca—piano
　　　　　　Jacob—dishes (with Mom's help)

7:45 A.M.　Jacob—piano

8:00 A.M.　Junior high schoolers leave

8:15 A.M.　Elementary schoolers leave

8:30 A.M.　I leave for work (in the Franklin Day Planner
　　　　　　bookstore)

2:00 P.M.　I come home from work

2:45 P.M.　Kids are home from school

3:00 P.M.　Joseph, Rebecca, and Jacob fold clothes from the
　　　　　　morning's laundry and put them away

3:30 P.M.　School preparations (homework, tomorrow's attire,
　　　　　　music lessons, athletic practices)

5:00 P.M.　Dinner and dishes (dishes done by the kids on a
　　　　　　daily rotating basis)

6:00 P.M.　School preparations and free time

7:30 P.M.　Showers and preparations for bed, including a final
　　　　　　pick-up of the house by everyone

8:00 P.M.　Bedtime

I read this schedule now, and I have to admit that I am amazed
at what was accomplished. I now understand why motherhood is

an occupation for the young. Following such a schedule took a constant infusion of energy and concentration. There were times, even with our daily planning, and everyone's schedule written down in my day planner, when preoccupation with dinner or visitors would cause me to forget a pick-up, a practice, or a music lesson. Despite the inevitable glitches, I try to think of accomplishing what we did without planning and scheduling. It could never have been done.

Building in Flexibility

We have had people tell us that the whole idea of the Magic Three Hours is unrealistic or that they find it intimidating. As our practice has become more widely known, people have admitted that they have actually driven by our home at 5:30 A.M. just to see if the lights were on.

I can only report that this approach has worked for our family. I recognize that it may or may not fit in with the dynamics and relationships of other families. The important thing is to determine what kind of program *will* work for you and your family, one that will help teach children the value of work and other important values that we can no longer be sure they will absorb from society, school, or modern-day family experiences. Who among us, upon seeing a child about to dash into the street or fall into a pool of water, will not immediately respond to rescue the child from danger? Today's dangers are not so apparent, but they are no less real. If a structured program like the Smith family's Magic Three Hours can help your family avoid some of those dangers, use it. If something else is needed in order to accomplish the same thing in your family, by all means, use that.

I don't imagine for a minute that one plan will ever work for every family. But the principles of planning, setting goals, and building a schedule that facilitates reaching those goals are broad enough that almost any family should be able to adapt to them.

The important thing is to not leave the necessary teaching and transfer of important values to others or to chance.

Another clarification I should make is that although we were systematic, we were not inflexible. For example, my journal records one winter in Portland when, for six and a half solid months, someone was ill every single week. There were mornings when we were so tired after a late night that we would get up, say our prayers together, and just climb back into bed for another much-needed hour of sleep. That was just a simple matter of being perceptive about our own feelings and physical needs as well as those of the children. The important thing was to keep alive the spirit of what we were trying to do. Through the difficult times, being flexible allowed us to do that.

People have asked if our children didn't rebel at this schedule. They didn't, really, although there were times when one or another of them was less than enthusiastic about the program. This was especially true after they were old enough to realize that their friends were not necessarily doing the same thing in their families. In those scattered instances of questioning, I trusted the children and tried to help them see the right vision from within themselves.

For instance, when Glenna was a tenth grader, her best friend, a team member in basketball and volleyball, was stunned at Glenna's schedule. I remember the day Glenna announced to me, "I don't want to get up in the morning and study scriptures and practice the piano. Jenny doesn't. Why should I?"

I simply said, "Glenna, it's your decision. Why don't you check out of the Magic Three Hours for a while and see what you think."

In three days, she came to me and said, "I can see for myself that I'm losing out. I want to do it again." She loved her music, she loved sports, and she loved to do her best. The structure of our family life helped her do that. And because of her experience, she was a great fan of the system. If any of the other children thought about checking out, I never knew about it. I think Glenna just took care of them.

Many motivations are intrinsically built into a planned system like the Magic Three Hours. I believe that if the atmosphere is provided, the children will see the vision within themselves and become self-motivated.

Weekly Planning

We tried to simplify our busy schedules by taking time each Sunday to review our progress. The first Sunday of the month we would talk about our entire month, and each subsequent Sunday we would go over schedules and plan for the upcoming week. During these weekly planning meetings, we wore comfortable, casual clothing and created a relaxing family atmosphere. This meant we had no visitors, took no phone calls, and encouraged a leisurely conversation that involved all the children.

We began each planning meeting with prayer and scripture reading. After that, the agenda was very loose. This was a time for the children to vent any frustrations with school, schedules, or each other, and to express their disappointments and successes. We discussed school projects, specific challenges and needs, family problems, and ideas for the future. This forum gave us as parents the opportunity to share principles and experiences with our children. One rule did wonders toward keeping the atmosphere pleasant: No one could pass judgment on another, but everyone could offer suggestions that might help correct a problem. We tried to keep each meeting a positive, growing experience. Sometimes we struggled, but most of the time we succeeded.

After our open discussion, we all opened our day planners and reviewed everyone's schedule for the next week or month, highlighting the activities that we could all attend to support one another. We finished our meeting off with the traditional Sunday taco dinner, which everyone helped prepare. Our kitchen never seemed quite large enough, but we all crowded in happily, one grating the cheese, another slicing tomatoes and lettuce, others warming up the refried beans, cooking tortillas, setting the table, and making the drink. This was everyone's favorite meal of the week because it involved so much pleasant interaction and did not, like most other evening meals, have a scheduled deadline with other tasks. The kids and I also loved it because Hyrum always did the dishes, scouring the pots and pans and leaving the kitchen sparkling to begin the new week.

People have been astonished that we were willing to spend such a huge chunk of time every week on planning. Granted, planning was the agenda and the stated purpose, but our real goal was to spend time working together, learning to set goals and to see each other as resources. Yes, we made sacrifices; Sunday afternoons weren't a time for going off with friends, joyriding, skylarking, or goofing off. That didn't mean our Sundays were grim, though. A by-product of our spending a lot of pleasant time together was that we *liked* to spend time together.

Another valuable thing that came out of our Sunday meetings was that each child felt important because he or she was obviously and conspicuously a contributing member of our family organization. No family decisions were made without consulting the children in this type of setting—and that means all kinds of decisions: going into a new business, accepting a new Church calling, considering what kind of a new car to buy. Allowing the children to report on their week kept us in touch with their interests, successes, and frustrations. When one child was harboring bitter feelings about not getting a part in a school play, for instance, we could listen supportively and take advantage of a teaching moment to help her move toward understanding.

During these meetings we also communicated to each child, simply by discussing his or her plans and goals, that the activities each was involved with were important and valuable to all of us. Finally, coordinating our schedules and discussing the family's needs on a regular basis created an atmosphere of cooperation and flexibility. Being aware of what was going on enabled us to be more supportive of one another's needs.

August's Mega-Planning

Organizing our year was a major event that became something of a ritual. We incorporated an annual planning session, keyed to the school year, on the first Sunday in August. By then I had collected the school schedules and knew which days school would be out over the next year. The children were also expected to bring to this meeting their own school schedules, including athletic seasons and sessions, dates and times for music lessons and church events, a prospective budget, and any other important dates or items of which we needed to be aware.

We used a notebook or calendar to record our plans before the Franklin Day Planners became part of our lives. After their creation, however, we made sure that each of the children had a full day planner, complete with addresses, key information, finance planning, and pockets for pictures and identification.

For this mega-planning meeting, we would gather around the round table in the library, with snacks and juice on hand. We began with a prayer and then started into our session, which would often last a full morning (sometimes longer, if we got involved in gab sessions, storytelling, or serious decision making).

First, we would set our yearly goals, both personal and family, in five categories—spiritual, physical, cultural, financial, and educational goals. Each year we chose a book of scripture for daily reading: the Old Testament, New Testament, Book of Mormon, or Doctrine and Covenants. We also chose a literary classic that we would read as a family during the next summer. Glenna, the designated reader by choice of the other children, kept us enthralled with her dramatic renditions of Mark Twain's *Tom Sawyer*, Owen Wister's *The Virginian* (my own teenage favorite), John Fitzgerald's *Papa Married a Mormon*, and everyone's favorite, F. Hopkinson Smith's *Peter, A Novel of Which He Is Not the Hero*.

Then we branched out into a new skill. Often it was a new sport, such as tennis or archery. One year we all took violin lessons. (Some liked that well enough to continue even past the year.) Often it was a new household skill, such as sewing (everybody sewed at least one item of clothing) or cooking. Joseph locked in to cooking, developing his own specialties: biscuits and gravy, chicken Dijon, and barbecued ribs. One year we learned to crochet, with private lessons offered by an expert, Mother Ruth. When Becca was twelve years old, she began to crochet an afghan for me. Twice a year, while we are watching LDS general conference on television, she brings it out and works diligently on it. After eight years, she's very close to having it finished. I keep teasing Becca that I will probably be dead before I get my afghan, but she keeps plugging away at it.

One year our family skill was bread making. I had learned to bake bread years earlier at a Relief Society homemaking night and had continued to do it regularly. This year, however, the whole family wanted to learn the skill, so we built the job into our Saturday routine. We had a mill that ground our whole wheat into flour and aided us materially in the mixing of the dough. We would bake the bread in batches of eighteen loaves at a time, using a collection of assorted thirty-two-ounce juice cans standing upright in the oven. This was enough to feed our family for two to three weeks, with a few extra loaves for the neighbors. We often saved out some dough for scones or pizza crust. Each one had his or her specific job: measuring the ingredients, mixing them, greasing the pans, and, of course, laying out the butter, honey, and jam with which we would eat the results. This was a tradition that found a permanent place in our family lifestyle. As the older children left home, the younger ones took on new jobs in the family assembly line. As a result, all my children, boys and girls alike, can make a mean loaf of bread. That project was good, both for the body and for the soul.

We also selected several service projects that we would work on together. As an example, we took over seventy-five-year-old Mother Ruth's yard work during the summers we lived nearby in Centerville. This was quite a project, especially considering the turbo-speed growth of the thick lawn on her half-acre plot, and the fact that our job had to pass her exacting inspection. We would cut the grass, trim the edges, rake, sweep the walks and driveways, weed the garden, and start the water. It was a good two-hour project with all of us working, no matter how we divided it up. When Mother Ruth asked, we would also help her do the big cleaning inside the house: washing windows, moving furniture, vacuuming under the beds, or cleaning in the places that were too high or too low for her to reach.

Another service project we did as a family was to pick up the trash at the local elementary schools. It seemed that every school had its particular weak area in which trash built up. At Poinsettia Elementary in Ventura, California, it was the ramp leading onto the school grounds from the dead-end street. Children deposited their candy and gum wrappers and unwanted school papers there before entering or leaving the school grounds. At Reading Elementary in Centerville, Utah, trash piled up against the chain-link fence north of the playgrounds—always in hidden spots just out of reach of the teachers' eyes or the busy janitors' cleaning schedules.

One of the highlights of our mega-meeting was planning an annual summer vacation and how we would earn money to finance it. We established some ways in which the children could earn money for personal spending or for the vacation. For example, there was office work to be done for Hyrum (answering the telephone, filing, collating seminar manuals, typing, or entering data on the computer), as well as the more traditional neighborhood baby-sitting and yard work.

Next, we would go over with all the children some of the things that would be expected of them, based on their ages. We discussed what sports they might pursue, and what musical options or special interest classes would be available. We helped the children set goals for their grades and let them decide what chores they wanted to be responsible for that year, taking into consideration individual schedules and time demands. All the children played soccer, basketball, volleyball, and baseball, keeping them active in sports year round. We estimated practice times and lengths, and found the best slots for homework. After we discussed all the activities each child would be involved with and the daily chores that needed to be done, they collectively decided what time they needed to get up that particular year to accomplish their daily goals.

We planned our family budget and helped the children establish their own budgets. We asked each child to forecast expenditures throughout the year for such things as school fees, lunches, clothes, athletics, music lessons, and birthday and Christmas gifts for family and friends. Beyond this budget allotment, each child received an allowance—based on age and circumstances—for consistent completion of household chores. Of this amount, the children paid 10 percent for their tithing and an additional 10 percent to their savings accounts. The rest of their allowance was theirs to spend or save at their own discretion; they were responsible to handle both their budget allotments and their allowances appropriately. A milestone that made seventh grade special was getting their own checkbooks and assuming the responsibility of accounting for their expenditures to Hyrum at a month-end checkbook balancing.

An important assignment, and one that required a lot of discussion, was apportioning out the household chores to be performed each morning. There were bathrooms to clean, breakfasts and lunches to make, dishes to clear, and vacuuming to do. We laid out the list of chores to be done and, as much as possible, let each child choose his or her preferences. This technique was a good corrective if someone wanted to complain later about being the most overworked person in the family. It went without saying that each person was responsible for keeping his or her own room tidy, keeping personal items out of the family areas, and keeping items he or she used in the family areas (such as sheet music) neatly arranged. Each person had a dish-duty night, depending on practice schedules or other demands on their time. Mondays through Fridays were dish nights for the kids (Jacob was usually assigned to help one of the older children), and Hyrum and I took the weekends. The children kept their assignments for the whole year, taking pride in developing quality and quickness. Joe became such an outstanding breakfast cook that he volunteered for the assignment two years in a row.

We also chose one day each week, usually Fridays, for "Super Housecleaning Day." On that day we dusted and vacuumed the whole house; swept, mopped, and waxed floors; periodically washed walls and windows; and tackled other deep-cleaning projects. To make our Fridays more enjoyable for everyone, we always did something fun as a family in the evening. Whether it was going to a movie, going out to dinner, renting a video, or getting ice-cream cones, we all had something to look forward to after our big cleanup efforts.

Saturday was the children's day. This was the one day they could spend entirely as they wanted: sleeping in, playing ball, shopping, going out with friends, or whatever. Most of the time, Saturday was filled with various soccer or basketball games, but such involvement was always by choice. Saturday was also a well-deserved "date night" for Hyrum and me.

Sundays always consisted of church, our planning meeting, and the traditional taco dinner. The children were learning communications and planning skills, but more importantly, these Sunday sessions were a time to mobilize everyone's energies and commitment to maintaining our family lifestyle. The Magic Three Hours wouldn't have been so "magic" without this weekly meeting.

Mondays were always family home evenings. We scheduled no meetings, practices, or lessons for that night. After supper, our home evenings provided a leisurely and fun time for all of us to be together, with everyone participating in some way, conducting, singing, reciting, giving a lesson, or praying.

Another aspect of our mega-planning meeting was a run-through of the holidays and school vacations for the upcoming year. We planned what we could do together as a family on those days: spring cleaning, baking bread, updating photo albums, visiting grandparents, or going on a hike or camp-out. Every child was responsible for something on our outings: games, snacks, books and stories, audio tapes, songbooks, or coloring books and crayons. The children were never at loose ends when a school holiday came, and we didn't have problems with bored youngsters or idle teens drifting into trouble.

During the summer months, each child had an assigned day of the week on which he or she was responsible for all three meals, from the menu planning to the shopping to the cooking to the cleanup. Usually I took the assigned weekly shoppers with me grocery shopping, and the other kids gave them shopping lists to cover their menus. This shopping spree was an enjoyable time for us. I would play a game with my little designated shoppers, giving each child a verbal list of three or four items to pick up. They had to remember the assigned items and carefully compare prices to get the best value. The children enjoyed finding "bargains" and learned some math skills at the same time.

Washing the cars and mowing the lawn were summertime additions to the usual chores. Summer was also a good time for more time-consuming projects, such as sorting, indexing, and cataloging all the music in the house, or sifting through closets and drawers for outgrown clothes to be handed down or given away. Other projects included filing family photos, planting and weeding in the garden, and cleaning and organizing our growing library. Summer was a time for large-scale activities, and all the time we were having fun.

The process of reaching goals and accomplishing the tasks we had outlined for ourselves was indeed a process, not an event. Events like our planning meetings and our Magic Three Hours were a lot of work, but they were worth it. We knew that the better we planned and the more organized we were, the more we could get accomplished. The mega-planning meeting gave us the bigger perspective into which to fit our weekly planning and our daily implementation. This system has proven invaluable in extending the shadowfall of our beliefs and values into the hearts of our children.

Weave through my branches

People often ask us how our children felt about the Magic Three Hours and our structured household programs. It seemed only fair to invite the children to respond personally. So in 1990, when I began writing this book, I asked my children to reflect on their years of participating in the Magic Three Hours. I specifically asked them to express honestly their frustrations, successes, negatives, positives, failures, and accomplishments. All the children's responses had some elements in common: the early hour of rising, the individual prayers with us, scripture reading, household jobs, athletics, and music practicing. But they all had individual perspectives as well. These accounts are important because they make the process real, going into the details of the Magic Three Hours as experienced by the participants. I have presented them here in the children's own words so that you might better understand and feel the personality of each child.

Glenna

As far back as I can remember, my mother has awakened us early. Although the magic three hours wasn't named such until after I was in high school, it has always existed. When I was very small, the hour of beginning was 6:30 A.M. As we grew older and more involved, the time was pushed back a half hour every year. By the time I was fourteen, 5:00 A.M. was the time to arise.

My mother had various methods of waking us up. I can remember being jolted out of bed by the soundtrack to *Star Wars* played at 80 decibels or more. A more frequently used ploy was singing the BYU Cougar Fight Song as she came into each of our rooms. When I entered high school, I acquired my own room (for which I was eternally grateful), but it was in the basement, two floors below anyone else. So my mother invested in an intercom that had the most obnoxious, high, piercing "beep" ever heard. Every morning at 5:00, she would beep that thing to wake me up. I got so that I woke up at ten minutes to five every day and just lay there in dread, waiting for that beep to shatter the silence. My father was just as effective with his bugle, or with his irritating habit of ripping off the covers—all of them.

Of course, bedtime was at 8:00 P.M., which was the cause of wonderment, awe, and even ridicule by my friends, but believe me, by the time 8:00 rolled around, I was ready to go to bed.

And just what did we do when we were up? Well. The schedule varied from year to year. Reading the scriptures as a family has always been a given, as was practicing the piano. There were also various household chores to be performed. Every year our house "jobs" were rotated. One of us would have the laundry, which had to be done three times a week; one of us had the vacuuming. It seems we've always had a house with a lot of square footage carpeted. Nevertheless, that was the job I preferred, since it only had to be done once a week. My mother was kind enough to give me that job my senior year since I had already proven to be too busy with school and extracurricular activities to do a very good job at anything that required consistency.

When I was in high school, the job of making breakfast was delegated to my brother Joseph. Of course, it followed that the morning dishes belonged to either my sister or brother just younger than Joe. Joseph became an excellent cook. He cooks better than I do, which actually doesn't say much. My grandpa gave him a real chef's hat once, which he was proud to wear. Hence, the job of making breakfast became a job of honor—and one to be sought after by my younger brother and sister. Finally, the "mantle" of the breakfast maker was passed on to my sister Rebecca. Breakfast time became a grim experience for a while, but she eventually mastered the art. She and Joseph now team cook on many occasions. But, it must be kept in mind that they were only nine or ten when this began. Now the honored position rests upon my youngest brother, Jacob, who is twelve. He has not yet mastered the art, but I'm sure that with practice, he'll catch on.

The most despised job was cleaning the bathrooms. Every year we had to draw straws to see who would be the lucky one. Everyone was assigned a room in the house, besides their own, to maintain, and everyone had one night a week for dish duty. Sunday was always Dad's day since it was pretty well guaranteed that he would be home. It is still the case. Sunday is also the day we have the biggest meal. During the summer, the day we have dish duty is also the day we are responsible for the meals. Needless to say, we don't eat very much during the summer.

Obviously, all of these jobs can't be done within the literal magic three hours (which are between 5:00 and 8:00 in the morning), but the concept of the three magic hours carries through all hours of the day: discipline in doing what has to be done to keep the wheels turning, so to speak, and to achieve whatever goals have been set. Of course, growing up, I didn't realize that this was what was happening. Since it started when I was very young, it never occurred to me that there was any other way until my friends informed me that there really was an alternative route. A few of them thought that my parents were running an army and were secretly planning to break off from the United States to create an independent state.

In high school, my bedtime was moved to 9:00 P.M., due to the fact that I was so involved in everything. I think I tried everything at least once. There were volleyball and basketball practices on top of play practices, madrigal rehearsals, track, tennis, soccer, jazz band practice (I was the pianist there for only a short time), and . . . homework. By the time I was a senior, it finally occurred to me that

I couldn't do everything and expect to stay healthy, so I cut back considerably on the number of things I was involved in, but it was still enough to make the head spin just a little at times.

Another important part of the week was our "Sunday raps." This was a grueling two hours or so where we would gather with our day planners in hand to plan and coordinate our week. It was designed so everyone would know what everyone else was doing and when. At the time, the only productive thing about it for me was finding out who could trade on my dish night if I knew I wouldn't be able to do it. Otherwise it was tedious and time-consuming. I always had something else I felt I needed to do, or a friend that I wanted to visit, so of course I felt that we could have accomplished what we did in half the time it normally took us. But we were always hindered by sidetrack conversations, or everyone talking at once.

Nevertheless, scheduling was very important and often very tight. All six of us took piano lessons and we all had to practice in the morning before we went to school. There was no time to do it after school because of the extracurricular activities that everyone was involved in. That meant that at least two of us had to practice at the same time. So my parents took me down to the church house at 6:00, and while they played basketball with some men from the neighborhood, I practiced the piano in the chapel. That worked fine until I was kicked out by the janitor. Apparently, he felt it necessary to clean the church, and particularly the chapel, at that time in the morning. It ultimately worked out for the best because we found a white grand piano for an amazingly low price to take some of the burden off our faithful old upright that's about seventy years old. We put one piano upstairs and one down, and they were used simultaneously.

I am in college now—a music college, even—so the practice has paid off. But as I look back and think about what the magic three hours has achieved for me, my siblings, and my entire family, I think the most important thing is not the self-discipline it developed, nor the ability to organize, but the unity it created among the members of my family. The memories I have of my family planning together in the mornings, even when it wasn't pleasant, of working together toward a common goal, of reading, playing, and just being together mean more to me than anything. I appreciate the fact that my parents place a high value on my family being together in everything because, ultimately, my family is who, when life gets rough, will be there to stand up and admit they know me. I value the knowledge that, no matter what, I have a solid support system. My family knows what I want and what I am trying to achieve, as I know what they are striving for—and we support each other.

I would give anything to be able to go to bed at 9:00.

Stacie

What do I think about the magic three hours? What do I really think? I think it's pretty crazy. But I believe in it. Like most things in life, it's harder when you're in a situation to see what's really happening, what you should do, etc. And then when it's passed, and you look back, you can see exactly how things should have been. The answers are there now that the experience is past. But then, isn't that what gaining experience is all about? Boy. I'm an awesome philosopher.

Really, though, somehow this is kind of how I feel about the magic three hours. It was harder when I was going through growing up with the magic three hours to see the value of it. Luckily, I was sensible enough to trust in the wisdom of my parents. For me, that experience is invaluable.

Honestly, wouldn't you feel blessed to be born into a family that catapults you from sleep at 5:00 A.M. to study, discuss, practice, and collaborate? We're talking every school day of the week, without fail. What a blessing. (Futile attempt at humor.) I remember waking up at 4:50 A.M. thinking, "What if, just what if Mom let us sleep in today?" I would pray with all my heart, "Oh please, oh

please, let today be the day." But it never was. Mother would faithfully make her rounds. She would come in all cheery and happy.
Don't you just love cheery, happy people at 5:00 A.M.?

She would get us up and pray with us. We needed prayers.
Then we would all meet in the study room. We all looked like we'd
been fifteen rounds. We would read and plan, then practice our
musical instruments so that we might be talented people. At that
time, I didn't see the real purpose to this grueling schedule except
that it was a great source of attention with my friends.

Now I do. I remember when I went to college thinking, I can
arrange my schedule so I can do what I want, including sleep.

But the first little while at college was so mediocre. I kept thinking, "What's wrong? I never have time to get ready or do this blah,
blah, blah." I would call home and Mom would tell me to stick to
the basics and to start doing what I had been doing before. So I
began to do it on my own. Yes, me. And I felt so good. There's
nothing that feels better than when you feel you have accomplished
something—even simple things. It does wonders for self-image. I
would arise at 6:00 A.M., study, prepare for the day, occasionally
exercise, and then the rest of the day was mine for fun stuff. It gave
me a great incentive to get to bed at a decent hour as well.

Looking back at it, it is these times with my family growing up
that I remember. It has made such a difference in my life. I know I
can do anything and become anything because of what I learned
in those three hours each day. They are precious times. Family is
what it's all about, and I've been able to spend as much time with
my family as the average person might in three lifetimes. These
magic three hours have provided me with great lessons of life:
priceless values and good communication skills. I thank God every
day for parents—and especially a wonderful mother—with vision
and love enough for me to make this system a priority. So truly I
am blessed. Perhaps it is crazy, but it's so worth it.

Sharwan

"The Magic Three Hours"? Hah! I have to admit that sometimes I looked at it as the dreaded three hours. Of course, the dreaded three hours, for me, consisted of arising at 5:00 A.M., scripture study and "planning and solitude" from 5:00 to 5:30, piano practice from 5:30 to 6:00, followed by breakfast, doing household chores, and getting ready for school from 6:30 to 7:20, at which time I would either catch the bus, snag a ride, or, when old enough, drive myself to school, which began at 7:30. I was almost always tardy.

I called it the "dreaded three hours" because of the time at which it began. I used to wake up early and anticipate my mother turning on the hall light and then either my dad or mom coming down the hall to wake me up. I remember thinking that I was literally going to die from being so tired in the morning—and I would tell my parents that, too! But, I swear, they never believed me. I remember at times being so tired that I used to dream on purpose that my mom let us sleep in until 6:00. Then, at 5:00, when she really did wake us up, I would feel more refreshed. Sometimes at night, if I got to bed really late, I used to think, "Why bother going to sleep? Mom is just going to wake me up in five hours anyway." Isn't that crazy?

The funny thing is that on the days we didn't get up at 5:00 and we were lucky enough to sleep in, my mother would come in at 6:00 and say, "Okay, you guys, I let you sleep in, now we all need to pitch in to get everything done." That usually cracked me up because, normally, since I was expecting my mother at 5:00 anyway, I was already awake and couldn't fall back to sleep for that extra hour. Some sleep-in! What really cracks me up, however, is that we, as growing teenagers, looked at 6:00 A.M. as sleeping in. But I must say that on those days we did sleep in, nothing seemed to go right. We would miss our scripture reading and family bonding time and then I would have to find some time after school and basketball practice to practice my piano—which usually never happened. The whole day would go differently when we had one of our rare sleep-ins.

I look back now at that so-called three dreaded hours, and can definitely see why Mom called them the "magic three hours." What we accomplished in those three hours is enough to leave anyone in complete awe. A clean house, clothes washed, eight fed stomachs, six children all ready for school—four of whom had already practiced the piano for half an hour, spiritual growth and scripture study, and—of course—the day completely planned out as to who was going where and doing what, written down in every one of our Franklin Day Planners—all this before 8:00 A.M.

The lessons I have learned from this have already begun to pay off. There were times, I admit, that I wanted to quit piano and never take another lesson. There were also times that I wished I could be a normal kid and roll out of bed five minutes before class and still make it on time. And there were the times that I would look at my mom and dad at 5:00 in the morning and think, "They must be from hell!" But then they would kneel in prayer with me and my exhaustion would disappear, along with my orneriness at being awakened.

I am now a senior in college, attending Southern Utah University, majoring in communications. I have a minor in music and piano. Believe it or not, when I got to college I continued taking private lessons on my own, even though I swore up and down that I wouldn't. All those hours on the piano so early in the morning had paid off. I actually have some talent and received an award my junior year for my ability.

The scripture study has paid off as well. I have now read the Book of Mormon many times and have a strong testimony of its truthfulness. This testimony has seen me through many a hard day. I still read the scriptures daily because I have learned the value of reading them and the need for the words of the Lord to be taken into our hearts daily.

The family bonding time in the morning and the sense of

achievement from getting things done instilled in all of us a sense of confidence and high self-esteem. Each one of us has the confidence to dream and to go after our dreams.

My sister Glenna, who is a returned missionary from Italy, wants to be a concert pianist. In striving for this goal she applied to the Westminster Choir College in Princeton, New Jersey, and went there for two years. She is now at BYU majoring in music and doing very well.

My sister Stacie will be the first of the children to graduate from college this upcoming year. She is majoring in the social sciences. Stacie served a mission in England and married a total stud and is very happy.

My younger brother Joe was the star basketball player in his high school and is so good-looking he doesn't know what to do with himself. What is neat about Joe is that he tries to be humble and involve everybody. He just auditioned for his first play and landed the lead. Joe leaves on his mission in six months.

Rebecca, my younger sister, was the lead in her high school play and is involved with student government. She is also a star basketball and volleyball player. I get tired just watching Rebecca.

Jacob, my youngest brother, is "Mr. Read-a-new-book-every hour." He loves to read and is just starting to get involved in his high school.

And as for myself, I became the "Days of '47" Queen and the student body administrative vice president while attending SUU. I am currently preparing to leave for Bahia Blanca, Argentina, where I have been called to serve a mission. I now have the opportunity to go tell others of the "Magic Three Hours," and the importance of scripture study, family bonding, and personal improvement.

My parents have instilled in me values, for which I will be forever grateful. My family is awesome and it is because two people who believed in correct principles took the time and effort to make sure their children learned and came to believe in correct principles as well. I have a testimony of the "Magic Three Hours."

P.S. I hear that in the Missionary Training Center you don't have to get up until 6:00 A.M. I can't wait to get there!

Joseph

I never woke up at 5:00 A.M. to start the Magic Three Hours. My morning always started at 4:59 A.M. My eyes would watch the digital alarm clock by the door as one minute of pure agony and pain would begin to "tick" down. I would think to myself, "Maybe today will be different ..." But sure enough, before I could finish the thought the clock would change to the hour of 5:00 A.M. and the hall light would begin to flood through under my door. I could always hear my dad's footsteps coming down the hall. (I swear to this day he wore combat boots with the extra-thick sole so we could hear him coming.) He would get to the door, pause for only a moment, and then with great ceremony he would flip on the light. I think my room was the only one equipped with a flood-light. "Let the games begin!" I thought.

This is how every morning started for me. My memories include those of personal prayer with my father, family scripture study and planning, long piano practices, chores, getting ready for school, and playing tricks on my sisters while they were getting ready for school. On rare occasions I got to go and watch my parents play early morning basketball between 6:00 and 7:00 if I got my chores done early. However, the thing I remember the most was making breakfast. I don't know why, but year after year it was my job to make breakfast with my trusted assistant and lifelong pal, Rebecca. I loved it. Do you have any idea what it is like to make breakfast for eight people every morning, Monday through Friday? The menu had to be filling yet tasty, with plenty to go around. So we often had oatmeal and toast, eggs on toast, rice cereal, pancakes, French toast, hash browns (from potatoes left over from dinner), scrambled eggs, or cold cereal. Every once in a while we'd make our Specialité de la Maison—biscuits and gravy from scratch. Nobody makes better biscuits than me, and nobody makes better gravy than Becca. Nobody!

In conclusion, the Magic Three Hours taught me a lot of things. It taught me self-discipline, organization, in all honesty how to read, and the value of being prepared. Most of all, it taught me how important being close as a family really is. This space of time in the morning was sometimes the only moment my family was ever able to share time together. It was often the only time I got to see my father. That is why it was important to me—to get to know and be with my family. It is getting more and more rare to see a family that is really close, where everyone loves each other. A big reason for this, in my opinion, is because families today don't spend any time with each other. They don't read the scriptures together, they don't pray together, they don't eat together, they don't even spend time talking to one another. If nothing else, the Magic Three Hours strengthens the bonds of love in relationships between family members. I'm reminded often by a plaque above our table which reads, "A family that prays together, stays together." This is what the Magic Three Hours taught me.

Rebecca

What do the magic three hours mean to me?

If this question were to have been asked five years ago, I would probably have been very negative in my answer. Getting up so early wasn't really a cool thing to do, nor was having to be in bed early a great thing, either. It very much limited what I wanted when it came to my night life and trying to be the most popular girl in school. I felt like a big nerd. All of my other friends would tell countless stories of how they just got out of bed five minutes before the school bell would ring and they still had enough time to look perfect. Hair, makeup, and all! I felt so deprived. Why did I have three hours to make sure I looked perfect, and why was it that I had pretty much accomplished a day's worth of obligations all by the time I had gotten to school? How unfair not to be typical.

Now, the thought may be running through your head, do you know how many people would kill to have all of their chores and obligations for the day done by 8:00 in the morning? You see, it isn't until now that I recognize what an amazing trick my parents were teaching us. To someone in high school, fitting in means a lot, and getting up and going to bed so early wasn't the pinnacle of how to be accepted. But to someone who is venturing out into the world for her first time going to college, trying to get a degree, holding a job, or trying to make something of herself, the picture becomes all too clear. Because of those dreaded three hours every morning, I now know what it takes to remember who I am. My greatest teaching moments happened in those three hours. I learned discipline. I learned structure. I learned how to stand on my own two feet. I learned to appreciate my sleep. I even learned a little about cooking. (You see, miracles do happen.) Most of all, I gained an amazing appreciation for my family. Those three hours took all of us. We all had separate chores and duties, and at five in the morning, we came together to make it happen. If one of us was out of sync, we all felt it. We were like a machine, and to turn the machine and to let it function takes all the parts. I have never met a family that works together, plays together, and is so close as mine. I attribute my family's closeness to those three little hours we spent together every morning.

Sure, high school is a place to have friends and to fit in, but those friends come and go. The one constant that I know will always be a part of my life is my best friends, my family.

Jacob

I'm sitting here in my flat in Gloucester, England, and my mind goes back to all the mornings that you got us out of bed early. You taught us to read the scriptures, to plan our day, to pray, and to work.

All those mornings you or Dad would come in at 5:00 and turn on the lights, and I would groggily roll out of bed—those are the things I'm grateful for now. Every morning I get up, bathe, plan my day, read the scriptures. I guess the strangest thing now is that I love it. We (my companion and I) pray more now than I thought anyone ever did, and it truly helps us feel peace and happiness in our lives as young missionaries 6,000 miles from home.

The knowledge of the scriptures that I gained through the Magic Three Hours is my greatest ally. Every day, something that I studied in the past is a help, a strength. The scriptures give me something strong to stand on.

Thank you so much for all those mornings, for making me get up, pray, and study the scriptures. Thank you for giving me the strengths that I need the most now.

Our system isn't for everybody. Personality, circumstances, or different views of the universe will shade everyone's approach to the world of child rearing. But maybe you can see how parts of it would work for you, or how you can reach the same goal using different means. I think the key question is: What do you want for your children?

The world begins at home. Within the walls of our home, thanks to the threatened miscarriage that kept me in bed and taught us that children rise to great expectations, we learned that even little ones can demonstrate amazing competence. We structured a family life to teach them competencies in many areas, but also to teach life skills that were universally useful: goal setting, planning, reviewing, evaluating, negotiating with others, maintaining commitment, cooperating, and rewarding themselves and being rewarded for achievement.

From competence springs confidence in trying new things. And from ease with oneself and one's abilities comes the feeling of abundance that can overflow readily into compassion for others. Thus confidence, competence, and compassion, the qualities that we had hoped to help our children develop, were a natural outgrowth of the Magic Three Hours.

A thousand leaves

As Glenna so aptly explained in her evaluation of our parenting strategies, "the concept of the Magic Three Hours carries through all hours of the day." The habits of growth, discipline, and togetherness had roots in that morning time with our family, but many other settings and methods figured in our efforts to nurture those values.

Quality Time, Quantity Time

In the current parenting debate between quality time and quantity time, Hyrum and I come down firmly on both sides. We've sacrificed a great deal to put our children and each other first, but the reward is that we enjoy being with each other most of anyone in the world.

It's one thing to say we want to spend time together, and another thing to actually do it. We carefully chose activities we could do as a family and consciously made the time for them. Some fell naturally into our routine, like reading the scriptures together daily, discussing the characters and the stories, and then looking for opportunities to apply them in our lives. The children took their turns reading aloud; as a result, their reading skills were far advanced for their years. Helping the children with the dishes gave me other great opportunities for one-on-one time with them.

We planned for togetherness and worked hard to achieve it. Because of Hyrum's schedule, time with him was particularly precious. I always tried to arrange things so that I could take him to the airport and pick him up. If they weren't in school, the children accompanied us on these airport trips. Because Hyrum nearly always returned at night, it was easy for us to go as a family to pick him up, even if it was so late that the children had to go in their pajamas.

Getting a treat at the airport was part of that family tradition. The ultimate treat was to go to the Portland airport restaurant and have an Eskimo pie, which was a square of chocolate cake with hot fudge on it, and then ice cream with more hot fudge and another piece of cake on top. It was probably a dietitian's nightmare, but it was part of our family togetherness. We've tried Eskimo pies all over the world in an unsuccessful attempt to duplicate the ones we used to get at the Portland airport. Another fun treat was to park the car at the end of the parking lot and take the shuttle bus in, then go to Hyrum's gate and greet him as he got off the plane. It wasn't always practical, but we did that whenever we could.

On one 2:00 A.M. airport excursion as we waited in the car at the curb nearest the baggage claim, we saw a huge rat waddling obesely along the curb toward our van. It looked like Templeton from *Charlotte's Web* after his midnight foraging through the fair-grounds. We were relieved when the rat finally lumbered past the van; after that experience, we were especially glad to see Dad!

During the three years Hyrum was mission president in California, he had a heavy schedule of speaking on weekends throughout the region at firesides, retreats, stake conferences, special events, and priesthood meetings. Hyrum had the title, the authority, and the responsibility, but both of us considered it a joint effort. I accompanied him to many of his assignments and also spoke, if only a few words, at most of them. To keep our commitment to make weekends family time, we would piggyback activities on his schedule. Frequently Glenna, Stacie, and Sharwan—ages ten, nine, and eight—would sing trios or play the piano. People were charmed with their talents, and the children felt good about "helping Dad." Even Joseph and Becca, at age five or six, would sing short songs or speak for a minute or so. It was a way of keeping the whole family involved. If the nature of Hyrum's meetings precluded our direct involvement, we would research what there was to do nearby and enjoy that activity while he was involved with the group.

We made the drives to and from our assignments pleasant with car games, songs, stories, and treats. The children thought staying in a motel—especially one with a swimming pool—was the height of pleasure. And eating out, even if it was only hamburgers, made them feel special. If Hyrum and I were hosted at a dinner, they went with us, carefully using their best table manners.

Besides all the meetings and speaking engagements, we had the opportunity while in the mission field to visit such places as the J. Paul Getty Museum, Hearst Castle, several early California Spanish missions, the *Queen Mary*, Hollywood Boulevard, and even the Rose Parade. Our children always accompanied us to public events whenever possible. We took the time to spell out in careful detail ahead of time what we expected of them: what constituted acceptable behavior, what reward they would get if they met our expectations, and what sanctions there would be if they exceeded the limits. So they knew from the time they were little that it was okay to jump up and scream at a game, but not in a movie or at a museum. We didn't want to be anxious about their behavior, and we didn't want them to be anxious. Clear expectations made for an enjoyable experience all around.

Church meetings required some special thought; they present a big challenge in any young family's life. On the one hand, we felt that families should be together in church; on the other hand, we couldn't allow our children to disrupt the experience for others. Church is a place to be reverent, but it's difficult to convey that expectation to a tiny child. I thought through this situation carefully and decided that I would not let church spoil Sundays for my children. I came prepared with snacks that could be eaten with no mess, toys that would make no noise, and quiet books. That way the children could be with us, but we were not requiring them to pay attention to a meeting that was not designed to communicate with children.

It didn't always work, of course. All of my children have been warned during church that the foyer is not a place for running around, and that if I have to take them out of the chapel for misbehavior, they will be spanked. Every single one of them has tested that statement, been spanked, and learned that the foyer was not a play room. I know that some who sat near us shared the suffering and probably wished I had a different rule. But I took the risk to teach the lesson.

Hyrum was nearly always on the stand because of his callings, so we sat on the front row. Thus, even though Hyrum couldn't sit with us, he could see the children; occasionally a thunderous scowl from him would nip prospective misbehavior in the bud. And certainly, the great example that the older children set for the younger ones was invaluable.

A far-from-small side benefit of spending a lot of time together was the incredible loyalty the children developed for each other. We planned together, worked together, attended each other's games and performances as a matter of course, and included each other in our world to an extent that I think is rare in today's families. This loyalty shows up in little ways. Joseph, for example, has never been afflicted by the bashfulness most teenage boys exhibit at giving anyone in the family a hug or a kiss in public. During his Eagle Scout award presentation, the boys were expected to give their mothers a thank-you kiss. Kissing moms in public seemed to embarrass the socks off the other boys. Not Joseph.

Even more touching, Joseph insisted that Becca get an award that night too, because she had worked so hard and helped him so much with his Eagle project. Joe chose a gold medallion for her and had her named an "honorary Eagle Scout."

Spending quality *and* quantity time with children can be a demanding habit. One night at 1:15 A.M. our phone rang, waking us out of a sound sleep. It was Stacie, calling from her student apartment. My first thought was, "Is anything wrong? Is someone hurt?" Stacie was so excited that her words were tripping over themselves. Larry, the apple of her eye and the one for whom she had serious hopes for romance, had finally kissed her. He had come over with a friend, and they had just stayed and stayed and stayed. The friend at length had announced that he was tired and would wait in the car, but Larry had lingered at the screen door until finally ... She couldn't call us before now, but she just *had* to tell us.

For Hyrum, who had answered the phone, the first reaction was: "Stacie, that's great, but do you know what time—"

I practically shoved him out of bed with my foot. "Hyrum," I hissed, "if she's willing to tell us about it, we'd better be willing to listen!"

So we heard the whole thrilling account of Stacie's first kiss from her future husband. No, the timing wasn't terrific, but the experience was.

Managing Money

Hyrum and I have always had a strict budget and have tried to manage our money with the utmost economy. For most of our married life, being careful with our money has been an absolute necessity. This has not always come easily. Although we agreed early in our marriage that we would never go in debt for anything other than an automobile and a house, Hyrum and I started out with some fundamental differences in how we approached finances. In the early years, I was the one who established the budget and tracked the money in the checking account, and I had a hard time spending money on anything that wasn't absolutely essential. Hyrum, on the other hand, has always been generous by nature and was always making unplanned purchases when he became aware of a need or was impressed by a sales presentation. At the end of the month, I was frustrated at finding checks in the bank statement for purchases that I had not been aware of. As a result, I automatically cut corners and skimped in other areas to make ends meet. After some long discussions, we decided that Hyrum would take on the responsibility for budgeting and tracking our finances. After a month or so, he understood that we had only so much money at a given time.

Conversely, I have learned to appreciate Hyrum's foresight in making purchases that had a long-term benefit—such as a new sewing machine or a family entertainment system. I often questioned such purchases at the time they were consummated, but they made lasting and important contributions to our family. Not long after we moved to Portland, for instance, Hyrum came home one night with an expensive stereo system. Although I was initially frustrated by Hyrum's purchase, I soon came to appreciate his long-range wisdom. Not only did that purchase expose our children to good music, but the kids quickly learned that they could turn into performers by plugging in the microphone and singing along with the music. I suspect that the stereo system had more than a little to do with their discovery of their singing talents. Hyrum helped me realize that some purchases were important investments in our family's future.

During our student years, the G.I. Bill paid 250 dollars a month. From that amount we squeezed out rent, gasoline, and books. Both of us were resolved that I would be a full-time mom for Glenna, so my finding a job was not the option it was for many student couples. As Stacie and then Sharwan were born, also during those student years, no job on earth could have tempted me away from the three.

Somehow, in those lean times, we made ends meet—often thanks to my parents, bless their hearts, who kept us supplied with beef for the freezer, eggs, butter, and bottled fruit. When we visited St. George they would always load us up. We laughed about how, as students, we were too poor to buy chicken, so we ate steak instead. But there were plenty of weeks when our budget was no joke. Just after Stacie was born in 1969, we had hot dogs for Thanksgiving dinner. That was what we could afford.

We have tried to teach our children that money is never a possession, always an instrument. It's worth working for, not because possessing it is intrinsically important, but because with it many good things can be done. We taught them that society pays its respects in money, and that they should honestly earn what they receive, always remembering that money is their servant, not their master.

We had two methods for teaching our children to respect money without letting it dominate them. First, we taught them to pay their tithing, one-tenth of what they received. Another tenth was to serve as an investment in their own future in the form of a long-term savings account. It's hard to feel totally possessive about money when you have already mentally distributed part of anything you will receive.

The second strategy is to turn money rapidly into rewards, so that money itself does not become attaching. One example of working toward a financial goal that involved the whole family was our first super vacation, something the children still mention as a combination of sustained work and glorious fulfillment.

When we were living in Centerville in 1983, we decided during our August meeting to go explore Hyrum's roots. What would the children think about a super vacation—thirty days in Hawaii? They were wildly enthusiastic. St. George was like a second home to them, but Glenna, Stacie, and Sharwan had been toddlers when we had spent our one part-year in Honolulu. They all wanted to go see where Dad had lived and gone to school, and to meet his friends and associates.

We spelled out the conditions. Hyrum had accumulated enough frequent flyer miles to pay for four of the airfares, but we would all need to help come up with the money to purchase the other two tickets. So each child had to earn enough to pay for his or her share of the airfare, plus some for spending money, which we estimated at about a hundred dollars each. They were enthusiastic about that too.

We began seeking work opportunities. Mother Ruth introduced us to a friend of hers, Brother Bosic, who had a knife- and scissors-sharpening shop. He accepted a business deal we offered him: We would gather scissors from people in our ward and neighborhood, label them with little name tags, take them to Brother Bosic for sharpening, and then return them to the owners. He kept one dollar and we kept two. He also made wooden lawn ornaments, which the children sold throughout the neighborhood, again earning a commission.

The children searched high and low for odd jobs. They babysat, mowed lawns, raked leaves, cleaned garages, and put their housecleaning skills to good use for hire. Our day planner business was just beginning, and the children were our first assembly crew, collating the thirty-seven pages in the first simple manual and popping them into three-ring binders for ten cents a book. Stacie, age thirteen, took over processing the orders for a motivational book Hyrum had written, *Where Eagles Rest,* which we sold from our basement. Stacie took the orders and packaged up the books for mailing. We trained all the children to answer the telephone in a professional manner, since at that time it was also the business phone. We had rehearsals and drilled them in what to say, how to check Hyrum's schedule, and how to take messages. To prove we were serious, we rewarded them if we later got a compliment or positive comment about them. And if we scheduled a seminar as a result of following up on a call they had taken, we gave them fifty dollars.

An unbelievable invitation next came. The family who had purchased the home in which Hyrum had grown up was coming to visit family members in a town just five miles away from Centerville. Would we be interested in house-sitting for them in Hawaii? We would. Would they be interested in using our car while they were in Utah? They would. We were both delighted with our exchange.

The big day finally came, and we were off. We had planned to learn about Hawaii in particular and Polynesia in general while we were there. Each morning we followed our Magic Three Hours routine, then hopped in the station wagon and headed out. Each day included a visit to a monument, a library, a marine show, a museum, or an exhibition of a native craft. We learned to hula and to make leis. We inspected sea mammals and fish. Many of Grandma Smith's friends invited us to dinner or to family home evenings. We barbecued in the park, explored the beaches for seashells, and swam every day. Everyone learned to surf.

It was interesting to see how the children budgeted and spent their own money. Glenna methodically allowed herself only two dollars per day. On some days she would not spend anything, allowing her under her tightly formulated system to spend the money she had thus "saved" for an occasional larger purchase. Stacie spent as she saw and was out of money early. Sharwan spent her money on treats. Joseph, Becca, and Jacob were younger and deferred to Mom and Dad for most of their spending decisions. Everyone purchased school clothes at a Salvation Army store that offered great buys on goods donated by wealthy Honolulu residents.

It was a perfect thirty days. We came back with every child a believer in planning, working, saving, and savoring the pleasures of achieving a goal.

Rewards and Discipline

Our summer super vacations have been a great way for us to reward the children for accomplishing their tasks during the school year. Over the years, we've taken trips to Disneyland, gone boating among the red-sandstone canyons of Lake Powell, attended company outings, traveled to visit grandparents, and enjoyed a number of other summer family activities together, some as simple as camping in our backyard and sleeping on the trampoline.

But summer is often a long way away, so we used weekly rewards as well. As was discussed in greater detail earlier, Friday was our major housecleaning day and Saturday was reward day. If the children stuck to the schedule throughout the week and accomplished all their tasks, then Saturday was free time. They could watch television or go to a movie with friends or have friends over.

We tried to use natural consequences in providing motivation. Children who didn't do their jobs during the week *had* to do them on Saturday—no playing, no television, no movies. If the child was playing on a soccer team, he missed his game, letting down the team and depriving himself of an activity he loved. If we had a family activity planned, it would be cancelled for everyone. That may seem harsh, but Hyrum and I adhered to the idea that just as an automobile can't be driven with a flat tire, a family doesn't really function well without all of the family members participating—and that applies to family fun and rewards as well as to family responsibilities.

Of course, we had specific family rules with specific punishments attached. It may surprise some people that, for the most part, those punishments were determined by the children themselves. Once, for example, our children came up with the idea of "solitary confinement" for a particularly blatant violation of family rules. That meant being banished to an especially gloomy basement bathroom to spend a specified number of minutes thinking, with no books, no radio, just solitary silence. The kids even put a poster on the door featuring jail cell bars and a title: The Jailhouse. This turned out to be quite effective in providing a "time-out" situation, although we would never use it for extended periods.

An infraction of the rules might also result in "parole," which was similar to what some families would call grounding. Being on parole meant no playing with friends, no phone calls, no TV, and no outside activities. We seldom needed other measures.

And we didn't need even those sanctions very often. Positive results did most of the disciplining for us. Besides, one of our basic philosophies is that spending time together is in itself rewarding, because you're surrounded by people who know you, love you, demand the best from you, and support you.

Planting the Seeds of Work

I always knew where I stood with Pat Brewer, a dear friend in Portland, Oregon, who used to come to my house to give my children piano lessons. If I ever called her to ask a favor, when she could help me she would, but when she couldn't, she'd simply say, "Nope." No excuses or explanations. She was one of the first who rallied when my pregnancy with Rebecca kept me in bed. Pat was in her midthirties and married, but didn't have any children at the time. She later moved to Denver, where she had three small children of her own. We kept in touch, and during one of our phone conversations, Pat commented, "Gail, now I understand why your children's beds were always lumpy."

I said, "What do you mean, Pat?"

"Well," she explained, "when I used to come to your house, I couldn't understand why your kids' beds were always wrinkled or lumpy, even though they were made. I just couldn't understand it, and I judged you as not being a very good housekeeper. Now that my children are four and five years old, I understand why your beds were lumpy. You let your children make their own beds!"

I laughed at her tone of triumphant discovery and confirmed, "That's right."

She continued, "It's really hard for me to do that, because I want them made neatly and up to my expectations."

All mothers probably have that attitude at one point or another. It's easier just to do the work ourselves: the job gets done better and faster. Of course, Pat already knew the reason for squashing such an attitude of impatient expectations. The mother gets the work done but has to do it forever because, as she is doing the task, the children are learning that they are inadequate and incompetent. Furthermore, she has just handicapped herself in the other great battle we parents face in teaching our children how to work: getting the child to perform the work in the first place. We need to understand that it is through the process of allowing (and requiring) the children to work at their own level, to the best of their ability, that we teach them responsibility, self-satisfaction, and independence. They learn what it means to feel success.

In working with my children, I always spend some time thinking first—thinking about the child, thinking about the job, and thinking about my goal. I can't, for instance, have a goal related to an individual job that would conflict with our greater goal of shaping competent children.

I also think through the child's individual capabilities—age, skill, and confidence level. High expectations only work if the child can actually perform the job, and setting a child up for failure is a terrible experience for both the parent and the child. A mother well knows that each child in a family is different in temperament and abilities. For example, I could instruct one of my children to take a stack of folded towels upstairs and put them away, return two books to the shelves in the study, and hang up a coat that was over a chair—and that child would go and accomplish the needed tasks. On the other hand, another child, if given the same set of directions, would probably get sidetracked by a toy or a butterfly on an upstairs window sill. Still another would say she would do it, but I would have to follow up to see if she actually performed. Goals for each child must take such variables into consideration.

When I have those principles clear in my mind, I set up my expectations of what constitutes a "good" job and how I expect the child to do the job. For a child's first time tackling a new task, I work with him or her individually. I explain what we want the end result to look like. I give the child the "job description" as we work through it, making sure that the instructions are simple, well defined, and in a logical sequence. It is important that he or she have a clear understanding of the whole picture. Sometimes I make simple charts showing each step of the process. And I make sure that there are three incentives accompanying the job: the child's recognition of performing up to standard, my praise of his or her accomplishment, and a privilege or reward.

For example, when I taught six-year-old Jacob to clean the bathroom, we both went into the room and I announced enthusiastically, "When we're finished in here, the fixtures and mirrors will shine, the towels will hang straight, there will be no puddles or litter on any of the surfaces, and the wastebasket will be empty." This is the overview. It sets up six criteria, even if they aren't phrased quite like a list.

We grabbed the portable tote with all the necessary cleaning supplies in it, and together Jacob and I cleaned and polished the mirrors. Then we scrubbed and rinsed the sinks and bathtub. To clean the toilet (a skill Hyrum always demonstrated to the children), we used a different brush, cleanser, and technique. Jacob thought that was pretty neat. Then we wiped off the counters and polished them dry. The floor needed to be either vacuumed or mopped, depending on which bathroom it was. Next came the trash, and he already knew how to dump it in the garbage can. Then I showed him how to straighten the towels and refold any items in the linen closet that may have gotten rumpled or out of place during the week.

We repeated this process until Jacob could give me exact instructions about what steps needed to be done, in what order, and to what specifications. After a couple of times working with him, I announced, "Jacob, this is now your job. You're the boss of the bathroom. You're responsible for tidying it up every morning before breakfast, and giving it a good cleaning on Fridays. And I'm counting on you to do it." He nodded.

During the Magic Three Hours, I try to walk the fine line between observing and policing. If someone needs a hand, I'm there. When a job is finished, I try to show up promptly, put my arm around the child, and pour out a little praise. It makes both of us feel good.

We have a simple, four-point philosophy of discipline: (1) the best disciplinary agent is reality, (2) encourage choices but present choices between positives as much as possible, (3) share all the information you have, good *or* bad, and (4) evaluate the consequences, both for the short term and over time. As a result, the children learn to deal with the natural consequences of their stewardships. If Jacob does the job on time and well, he's a happy boy, I'm a happy mom, and the bathroom sparkles. If he doesn't, then we start with the expectations. Does he know the expected standard? If I've done a good job of teaching, he does. Usually, just looking at the room with him and asking him to tell me the six things that make a good job in the bathroom will solve the problem. In the rare instances when there is a problem with getting a job done, I've learned that it generally has nothing to do with the job itself. That's a time to sit down with the child, to talk, to explore feelings and try to understand the deeper problem the child is trying to deal with.

Another crucial point to remember—because it's such an ever-present temptation—is not to add on more jobs once a task has been finished according to the stated expectations. This is why I always think through what constitutes a good job ahead of time.

Perhaps it should go without saying, but I'm going to say it anyway: parents should teach children to work by setting an example. Our children were never asked to do anything that they had not seen us do many times. No child in our family has had the privilege of ordering a younger sibling to take on a job that she or he didn't want to touch. All of them worked beside me in the garden and the house, seeing order emerge, surfaces sparkle, and savory meals appear.

Spending quality time together, managing finances well, disciplining effectively, and teaching our children to work were all important values to us. Perhaps the greatest reward in all that we did to try to share those values was in the results that came from setting and achieving goals. By the time they were in fifth or sixth grade, the children were fully aware of how much they were accomplishing. They loved the sweet success that comes from achievement. They thrilled at their own skills and at their self-sufficiency. They were experiencing some of the rewards that make adults happy too—taking care of themselves and helping the people they loved. They had adult skills, like cooking, shopping, and earning and managing money. Success breeds success. No wonder they loved it!

11

Stirred in a thousand winds

The Magic Three Hours provide a wonderful opportunity for the consistent practice or development of talents and aptitudes. However, faithfully using this special time for such personal development does not provide any guarantee of success and fulfillment. When she was fifteen, Glenna learned this lesson in a most wrenching and unforgettable way for all of us.

Glenna had started picking out tunes on the piano when she was four, and a piano teacher in Portland appraised her aptitude and willingly took her on as a student at age five. For ten years, Glenna practiced the piano every day. She did it out of love; I never had to remind her. Our piano at home, a spinet, was scheduled every available minute by the younger children. So Hyrum and I would go to our local meetinghouse and play basketball in the gym with friends while Glenna practiced on the grand piano in the chapel.

For months Glenna had been practicing for a statewide piano competition. The story of that experience is best told in her own words:

The Piano Competition

I fumbled in the dark trying to find the lock on the chapel door of the church. I finally found it and went inside. I turned on one set of lights and looked at the clock. It read 6:05 A.M. I sighed as I walked up the aisle and on to the stand where the piano was. It didn't seem to get any easier. I could already hear my parents involved in a game of basketball through the wall in the gym.

I turned on the little piano light and turned off the big lights. This way I couldn't possibly waste electricity, as the janitor accused me of doing. He always gave me the same speech every day when I came to practice about how I shouldn't be here. "It's against church policy and it wastes electricity. We can't let everyone come here just to use the piano, and if we let one, we have to let all. Don't you have a piano of your own? I had five kids and put 'em all through piano lessons on one piano."

I had never heard of any such church policy. As far as electricity went, I used only a small piano light. Besides, what was the tithing and ward budget my parents paid used for? Didn't that pay for the light? And who else would want to come and practice on church pianos at six in the morning? I didn't believe him, but his obvious lack of welcome always took the edge of pleasure off my practice. I felt he just flat didn't want me there.

I had just finished my warm-ups and was starting on my real music when the door was thrown open and a vacuum was shoved in. Terrific. Mr. Janitor does it again. He always had to do the chapel first, out of all the rooms he could have started with. He had to come here first and spend nearly twenty minutes of my practice time vacuuming.

I played louder, not that it did any good. He always wore a Walkman radio and earphones in his ears. He was a big, tall, fat man with a gruff voice and baggy eyes. He'd been a janitor for twenty-five years. I kept playing Rachmaninoff as loud as I could while he brought the stupid vacuum up to the piano and literally vacuumed under my feet.

When he finally left, I was able to concentrate again on my music. I had two songs I was perfecting. Actually, it was too late to do any perfecting; this was my last practice before the statewide competition tomorrow. I was ready. I'd been working on this for the last two months. I had both my Rachmaninoff Prelude and my Bach memorized and had performed them for my teacher and various people several times.

I was aware of the doors being opened again. It was my mother. "Glenna, it's time to go." I looked at the clock. 7:07. I had to catch the bus to school by 7:25. I gathered my books together, put them in my bag, and walked out of the chapel.

The next morning, I woke early. Too early. I hadn't slept very well anyway, but it would have been nice if I could at least have dozed until I absolutely had to get out of bed. But here I was, as wide awake as anyone could be. I stayed in bed anyway until my mother came to get me up.

"What dress should I wear?" I asked, already knowing perfectly well what I wanted to wear. I would wear my purple dress, mainly because it wasn't black and I hated the fact that people traditionally wore black when performing in concert. Black was boring. Of course, this wasn't a concert, but close enough. Therefore, no black.

"Why don't you wear your white lace dress?" answered my mother. I hadn't thought of that.

"What about my purple one?" I countered. "It fits looser so it's not as hot."

"Wear your white one so people can look down and see a black grand piano and this person in white playing it."

My mother had struck the romantic part of me. I pictured a huge auditorium and a lone nine-foot black grand piano out in the center of the stage with a girl in white playing this gorgeous piece that everyone loved—and of course she won the competition. I wore the white dress.

I was scheduled to play at 11:20 and it would take two hours to get there through canyons and along one-lane highways. So the whole family—all eight of us, including Grandma Smith—piled into the green van at 8:30. It was the longest drive in history.

I wished that I had an earlier time. I hated waiting. It gave me too much time to think. This was my first competition since we had moved to Utah from California two years earlier. I played with my coat zipper. Up and down, up and down. It was about time I got a new coat. Nerves. Already I could feel the butterflies begin to arrive in my stomach. Why should I be so scared about the whole thing? I'd been in hundreds of competitions—well, quite a few, anyway. Was it just because I hadn't been in one for a while? No, I'd been in one or two recitals since—in my teacher's basement in front of her other students. But what if I drew a blank in the middle of one of the pieces? In the rush to leave, I hadn't brought my music. No, I willed, that wouldn't happen. I considered this as kind of a test or trial to prove to myself that I could still perform without major problems, or even minor ones.

"We're here," said my father.

Inside the building hung an air of tense excitement. Participants milled all over the place waiting for their turns to practice or perform in various rooms. Some were already finished and still had the rest of the day to wait for the results, telling them whether they had made the finals. Most were just waiting.

According to my schedule, the fourteen- and fifteen-year-olds were in Room 4. I first found where it was, then found an empty practice room.

Practice rooms weren't totally soundproof. You could still hear the person next door, and it wasn't exactly reassuring. I started right in on my Rachmaninoff Prelude in C-sharp. That was my favorite out of the two pieces I was doing. Besides, Rachmaninoff helped get rid of nervous energy. My other piece was by Bach. I liked Bach too, but the problem with Bach was that if you didn't have it learned backwards and frontwards, one finger played out of place threw everything off and you forgot where you were.

It was finally time. I sat outside the door marked 4 and waited until the person inside was finished. My whole family was with me. My teacher was there too, dressed in pants. Other people were waiting to perform with me. They all had their music with them.

"Myrtle," I asked my teacher, "was I supposed to bring my music?"

"I think so," my teacher said, alarmingly unconcerned.

"I didn't bring my music." I felt panic well up inside me.

"That's okay. If the judge asks you about it, just tell her you didn't bring it. She'll probably recognize what you're playing anyway."

Terrific. I was supposed to bring my music. Thanks, Myrtle. Maybe I wasn't as prepared as I thought. What if I drew a blank in the middle of a piece, despite how hard I'd practiced? No. I wouldn't do that. At least I wouldn't think about doing it.

The door opened, and everyone stood up to go inside. The butterflies had now all arrived in my stomach and were living it up while they had the chance. I was the last one in and the door closed behind me.

It was no auditorium. There was a black grand piano, but it was crowded against the wall of the long, narrow room, next to a brown piano. Five rows of chairs were lined up behind the piano so that the performers had their backs to the audience while performing. There was only one judge, an older woman who was running behind and wanted to get this group over with so she could go have lunch.

The girl before me went to her place at the piano. She had forgotten her music too. I felt a little better. The girl was playing the Grieg concerto, the same piece I had just started to learn. She played it flawlessly, a tough act to follow.

"Glenna Smith," called out the judge.

I stood up and made my way to the judge's seat.

"I don't have my music," I almost whispered.

"Well, what are you playing?"

"Prelude in C-sharp Minor by Rachmaninoff and Prelude in C by Bach."

"All right, I think I know those. Which one are you playing first?"

"Bach is first." I would do that one first so I could get it over with and relax with Rachmaninoff. I walked to the grand piano, wishing I'd worn the purple dress. I felt so stiff in the white one.

I started in on the Bach. I could hear every little whisper made by the audience, but I couldn't hear what they were saying. My mind began to wander. I wasn't doing so well in geometry anymore. They were starting to use algebra, which I knew practically nothing about. My cousin wanted me to try out for the high school madrigals as the accompanist. Maybe I would. I was only in ninth grade, though. Suddenly, I realized how little I was concentrating. I panicked. I was in a performance! I tried to bring my mind back to what my fingers were doing, but my fingers had been carefully playing along while my mind had been off in never-never land. Now I had no idea where I was in the song.

I stopped. My mind was totally blank. I started over, scared to death that I would forget again in the same place. Sure enough, when I got there, I went blank again. I tried again. No use. I couldn't remember anything past the first page.

"Why don't you go to your Rachmaninoff and then come back to this?" said the judge. Her voice was sympathetic, almost pitying.

I nodded and sat up straighter. I couldn't stand pity. I started Rachmaninoff. It was a deep, heavy piece with a lot of chords that used all ten fingers. It was a story about a man buried alive. The soft and dreary chords at the beginning told of the funeral procession making its way to the grave. The middle part was very fast, almost panicked, telling of the man in the coffin coming to the realization that he is about to be buried, so he starts beating on the inside of the coffin. No one hears him so he panics and beats harder and harder until the last part of the song is reached, which is chords again except loud and an octave apart. They gradually get softer and softer as the man becomes weaker and weaker. The song ends on a very soft minor chord as the man dies.

I barely heard the applause of the small audience. I had made it through without stopping. I waited until the judge was ready and then started Bach again. I made it through without forgetting anything.

"That's the way," said the judge. It sounded condescending to me. "It helps to play Bach after Rachmaninoff. You might try that next time."

My face grew red with anger and embarrassment. I got up from the piano with no expression on my face and made a deep, dignified bow as if I'd just been in a huge auditorium and had sat center stage at a long black grand piano, totally visible to all watching, in my very white dress. Then I walked out of the long, very narrow room that had two grand pianos crowded together as the first tears began to fall.

Hyrum, the children, Grandma Ruth, and I had sat frozen with apprehension during Glenna's performance. We were all hurting for her, but nothing like how my Glenna was hurting. She had wanted perfection in her performance so badly. Never in all her previous piano competitions had anything like this happened. Always she had come out a winner or with high marks. We did our best to cheer her up during the long ride home and she responded, on the surface at least, with a half-hearted smile.

In the days after the competition, my empathy button was ringing every bell in my body. I began at once to try to help her regain her confidence.

"Glenna, when a gymnast falls from the balance beam, she immediately gets back on the beam and begins again," I ventured. "Or when you miss a basketball shot, you don't quit shooting. Get back on the piano and play those two pieces." I pled, persuaded, begged, and bribed. Try as I might, I could not get Glenna to run through those two pieces. She continued her piano lessons and learned different pieces, but she avoided any retriggering of the horrible memory.

However, fate can sometimes turn even a searing failure into a success. Two years later, Glenna's English teacher asked her to enter a short-story writing contest sponsored by Brigham Young University. In her story, "The Piano Competition," she told of her agonizing experience two years before. The story (from which her words on the previous pages are excerpted) won the competition, and she received a fifty-dollar prize at the awards banquet. From Glenna's moment of failure had arisen a new talent—writing.

The next morning, as I was preparing for the day, I heard notes from the piano room. First, without hesitation, came the strains of Bach's Prelude in C, followed by the heavy Prelude in C-sharp Minor by Rachmaninoff. "Oh, thank you, thank you!" I said audibly, almost as if in prayer. "Rachmaninoff is still alive!"

Our children have had their share of elective success, winning various class and student-body offices in school. Those have been important opportunities to serve, to grow, and to increase in leadership skills. But the lessons from their defeats have been equally important.

When Joseph was in sixth grade, he ran for student-body president. He prepared thoroughly, organized a committee, campaigned hard, and put on a skit. He won easily in the primaries and looked like a shoo-in in the finals. But the day before the final vote, his opponent's mother died very suddenly from a heart attack or a stroke. Everyone felt so sorry for the girl that they voted her in. Joseph felt terrible that her mother had died and was filled with compassion because of her loss, but the defeat was a real blow to him. This mixture of emotions would be complicated for an adult to deal with, let alone a twelve-year-old.

It was a major topic at our weekly family planning meeting. We were able to acknowledge his conflicting feelings and discuss his situation. Just being able to articulate those feelings helped, especially since all of us had experienced losses and defeats of one sort or another. It was very helpful for him to realize that although he had not achieved something he desired, neither had he actually lost anything. In fact, he had gained. By organizing a committee and preparing his campaign and speeches, he had developed leadership and speaking skills that he could use on other occasions. With his feelings about himself in perspective, we could talk more generally about defeat and victory, life and death, and the death of a parent. All of us contributed. All of us learned. All of us grew.

Joseph needed that experience. He tried out for the school basketball team when he was in ninth grade and confidently expected to make the team, just as all three of his older sisters had. He was stunned when he didn't. It was a tough year for him, even though he got involved in the city league and was very successful. The next year, when he made the team as a sophomore, he was a very appreciative young man.

No recounting of our family's defeats and victories would be complete without the story of Sharwan, who became a rising star in her twenties after a challenging childhood and a cataclysmic adolescence.

Sharwan was different—in physical features, in temperament, in personality, and in intensity. Her will to follow her sisters and do everything they did was ferocious, but her little body simply lacked the skills sometimes. She was frequently frustrated and irritable. Glenna and Stacie were both anxious to please. Sharwan tested out exceptionally bright for her age but was headstrong, overreacting dramatically to stimuli. For instance, when she was six or seven, she was eating a boiled egg for breakfast one morning when she suddenly began screaming uncontrollably. She had bitten into her egg and a loose tooth had chosen that moment to come out. She completely panicked.

In school, Sharwan was always positive, aggressive, and competitive—and wildly popular—yet she needed constant reassurance and was always asking for approval. Glenna was always ready for a new experience. Stacie needed to be escorted to the door of her new classroom in the fall, but once there, a final kiss and a pat and she was over the threshold without a backward glance. Sharwan was always excited to go, but she would ask two or three times, "Mom, do I look okay? Is this blouse the right color? Is my hair all right?"

Always tall, during adolescence she outgrew her sisters as well as all the boys in her class. People—including us—sometimes expected seventeen-year-old behavior from a fourteen-year-old. She was compulsively tidy, organized, determined, and focused on her goals. These were good traits, but their down side was that she was also, during those naturally me-centered years, sometimes inflexible in her persistence. If she wanted something or needed to be taken somewhere, she hammered away relentlessly. She was a hard, fast, smart worker, but waiting for instructions was torture for her. Hyrum is an intense person too, and Sharwan's intensity clashed with his own.

In grade school, Sharwan discovered a lucrative racket. After a classmate had bought a nickel carton of milk with a dime or quarter, Sharwan would flash her million-watt smile and say, "How about lending me a dime?" or "I could use a nickel." She had squirreled away thirteen dollars before her sisters blew the whistle. Without overreacting, we sat her down, explained that what she had done was dishonest, and asked who had given her money. She has a great memory and was able to reconstruct the whole list. We had her earn the money honestly, then go back to each friend and return the money she had "borrowed."

Glenna and Stacie scampered to do Hyrum's bidding; Sharwan frequently wanted to argue, to know *why*. Unfortunately, she seemed to pick times when Hyrum was tired, when we were in a hurry to go somewhere, or when a series of unrelated events made her stubbornness the last straw. I sometimes went to bed exhausted from my peacekeeping efforts.

Talented and hopeful, Sharwan was devastated—as were we all—when she was not selected for madrigals her senior year after what seemed a successful audition. Another crushing experience came when, despite her height of six feet and her athletic ability,

Sharwan had a bruising year with an unsupportive basketball coach.

"I was the black sheep in the family," Sharwan remembered later. "Nineteen years old and my role in the family had been basically, as Dad puts it, 'a home-wrecker.' I had the self-esteem of a flea. I looked down on myself. I did not think of myself as a beautiful person inside or out." It breaks my heart to think of my wonderful daughter ever feeling this way about herself.

The turning point came over, of all things, a beauty contest. After high school graduation, Sharwan had a great freshman year at the College of Southern Utah in Cedar City. As a sophomore, she was president of Lambda Delta Sigma, the Mormon service unit on campus, and got a letter asking her to announce to her unit information about the pageant for the Days of '47 Queen. The glittering Days of '47 parade, held annually on July twenty-fourth to commemorate the arrival of the Mormon pioneers in Salt Lake Valley, is a legendary event in Utah. Its queen contest, sponsored by the Daughters of Utah Pioneers, requires that candidates be descendants of someone who crossed the plains before the completion of the transcontinental railroad in 1869. Sharwan announced the contest, but mostly to make fun of it. Still, the connection with pioneer heritage stuck in her mind. Mary Fielding Smith, her third great-grandmother, was a strong woman who brought a family of nine across the plains as a widow. She was five feet eleven inches tall, with dark hair, brown eyes, and a lovely singing voice. Sharwan realized that Mary sounded a lot like her.

She brought the application home. "Mom, what do you think?" Her voice sounded tentative and wistful.

"Great!" I all but shouted. "Definitely you should do this!"

She filled out her application. I looked it over before she sent it off and said, "Wannie, this is no time to be modest! Put down *all* of your achievements, *all* of your talents."

Reluctantly, she added more and mailed it off. I saw unbelieving delight on her face when the answer came back that she was qualified. Then she and I faced the gigantic problem: What next? My experience with modeling consisted of total trauma in Miss Marker's class. I could and did dress like a CEO's wife, but I had never bothered to study the fine points of elegance. My preferred outfit was sweats and gym shoes. I was out of my depth, big-time, in advising a daughter on charm, makeup, and wardrobe accessories.

Then an angel entered our lives. Eddie Ward and her husband, both dear friends, were with us as houseguests when Sharwan's letter came. Eddie had been in the same pageant as a high-school girl, and her sister had won the Miss Utah title in her own time. At that very time, Eddie's daughter was preparing for the Miss Salt Lake City pageant. Eddie was full of knowledge about what needed to be done and volunteered her unlimited services. Sharwan and I could only express our undying gratitude.

Right on the spot Eddie set up an appointment to go with Sharwan to purchase try-out clothes. Sharwan needed a formal gown to model for the talent show and a "Sunday best" outfit for the interviews. Eddie spent a weekend blitzing Salt Lake City stores with Sharwan, finding the perfect outfits and personally overseeing any needed alterations. The contest committee supplied information on the questions likely to be asked in the interview. Eddie drilled her, not only on the answers, but on how to speak. I had coached Sharwan in how to pivot, dribble, and shoot a basketball. Now Eddie coached her in how to sit, stand, and walk like a beauty queen. Sharwan also worked hard on physical conditioning, not only losing a few pounds, but toning herself into radiant and luscious health.

The day of the event came. Eddie had arranged an appointment with her own hairdresser, who piled Sharwan's hair in an elegant arrangement of curls and put on her makeup. When he turned her around to look at herself in the mirror, Sharwan's face stiffened. She quickly smiled and graciously thanked him, but as we walked toward the car, I said, "Wannie Bear, you seem disappointed."

She almost broke down. "Mom," she whispered, "this is just ugly. It's not me. It's a facade."

I took a deep breath. This was no time for panic. "Sharwan," I said as earnestly as I could, "this *is* you. And you *are* beautiful. This beauty business is something that you and I don't know anything about. It's time to trust the professionals. This man is a professional. He's assisted many queens. I saw how carefully he looked at you, how thoughtfully he made decisions, and how hard he worked. He wasn't just applying something from a book. He looked at your color, your face, and your hair. What he's done is professional. Let's just exercise faith."

Sharwan slumped in the car seat and nodded. Eddie had a set of last-minute instructions, did some last-minute coaching on the interview questions, and had Sharwan try on her day wear, making last-minute decisions on a couple of items. Sharwan felt better. After a special prayer, I drove her to the pageant site, registered her, and received the hostess's firm instructions that the interviewing was private and so was the first round of modeling in Sunday best. Families would be welcome in the auditorium for the final rounds and the evening wear modeling. I could pick up Sharwan for lunch at twelve, as long as I had her back by two.

At lunchtime, Sharwan was bubbly and excited. When I asked her how she was doing, she exclaimed, "Arghh! I don't know. I think it's out of my league. Did you know I didn't even bring a comb? Not even a lipstick!" Then she brightened and added, "But I'm having a lot of fun with the other girls."

After the afternoon round and dinner, the names of the final twenty were chosen and their families were allowed to be present. We clustered together anxiously, hoping for the best, fearing the worst. The girls were introduced by number only, lest a well-known family name subtly influence the judges or audience. I looked around the auditorium. Who were the parents of number 8, that gorgeous, petite blonde? I couldn't tell. Everyone looked proud. Everyone looked anxious. Sharwan's number, 27, always seemed to be the last one called as the girls modeled, answered a question, and waited for the announcement of the top ten.

I barely heard the questions that the judges asked in the final round of interviewing. I was dazzled by Sharwan's graciousness, her spontaneity and eloquence. She had never seemed so beautiful, her height adding a dimension of queenliness. The night before, Hyrum had asked her, "Why do you want to be queen? What could you give the people?" Sharwan told him, "The queen gets to speak a lot. It would be an incredible opportunity to share my testimony."

This was Sharwan's final interview question: "If you had to leave all you possessed to come west with the pioneers, would you do it, and why?"

As Sharwan recalled that moment later: "With all my heart, I said, 'I would. And I would do it to have the opportunity to share my testimony with others and build the kingdom.' It was the question that, without knowing it, my father had prepared me for. I think I felt the spirit of Mary Fielding Smith as I walked down the runway. I know I could not help smiling from the joy inside me. It was an incredible moment. Whatever happened in the contest, I knew I had already had my reward."

That's the part I remember: my Sharwan walking down the runway into the audience. She looked dramatic, her black hair glistening, her coloring enhanced by her white formal gown, her smile radiant. The anxiety I had been breathing past all evening simply and suddenly dissolved. I knew absolutely that Sharwan would be named queen.

That knowledge didn't stop my heart from racing as the final candidates sat, each exhibiting perfect poise under the scrutiny of hundreds of eyes. The judges announced their decisions: first alternate, second alternate, second attendant, first attendant ... I saw some of the children exchanging anxious glances. Sharwan's name had not been called. Did this mean she didn't even place?

Then the judge announced, "And as Queen of the Days of '47, number 27, Sharwan Smith!" The whole house exploded. It was as if everyone knew, everyone approved. The cheers and clapping were tumultuous. Sharwan's smile was brighter than the camera lights. As we swarmed around her on the stage, she threw her arms around me and bent to kiss me. "Oh, thank you, Mom," she whispered. "Thank you so much."

Tears welled up in my eyes, but when Sharwan turned to her father, and I saw the look on both faces as they embraced, I didn't try to keep the tears from spilling down my cheeks. I don't think they said anything. How could they have put into words what they were feeling? How often do you get to see a miracle right in front of your eyes?

I think the miracle came because Sharwan, for the first time, felt totally beautiful, inside and out. She felt right. She felt complete. She was not anyone's sister or anyone's daughter. She was herself and, just for a moment, she was perfect. She saw that perfection reflected in her father's eyes, and everything has been different between them from that time on.

When we got home that night, I looked at the biography of Mary Fielding Smith that Sharwan had been reading for a couple of months and caught my breath. "Sharwan," I called to her, "look at this." The portrait on the cover showed Mary Fielding Smith with her hair caught up in curls, exactly like Sharwan's. "Sharwan," I said, through my tears, "I know she was there, and I know there was a reason for all of this." Sharwan had felt the same way.

Now, one lesson from this experience, of course, is that it's important to find ways in which children can excel, so that each one can experience the thrill of succeeding in public and having others recognize that achievement. Behind an individual's growth is a parent's faith that makes the space for that growth. But perhaps equally important is the reminder that parents need to be humble. Even loving a child does not mean liking her, accepting her, or understanding her. Good relationships with two children do not guarantee an automatic good relationship with a third. Growth comes to parents too, line upon line.

When one is tall

Time and again, the simple and powerful faith of our children has thrilled and humbled us. Where we have lacked faith, they have shown us the way. Where we have hesitated and had doubting hearts, the path has been bright and clear before them.

When Glenna was about seven, we memorized a scripture in family home evening about making decisions. Doctrine and Covenants 9:8–9 encourages people to study out a decision, then pray; if it is correct, they will feel a "burning" in their bosom. If not, a "stupor of thought" will come over them.

The next morning, Glenna wanted to eat school lunch—pizza that day. I explained that I had no change to give her to buy school lunch and that I already had sandwiches made. She was willing to use some of her own money, so I told her it was her decision. I continued with the morning routine as she went downstairs to her room. A few moments passed. Then she returned and said, "Mom, I've decided to take lunch." She said she had applied the scripture she had learned the previous night and prayed about it. She said, "There really is a burning in your bosom when you know that something is right."

Now, whether she took a lunch or bought it at school was certainly not important. What *was* important was the faith of this young girl, and the experience she had in recognizing the feeling of the Holy Ghost.

Our children had many experiences with prayer, and have known the joy of having their prayers answered. One particularly poignant time that I remember was in connection with a soccer team. . . .

If only the game could go five minutes longer, I just knew the Pirates could score a goal. Alas, the whistle blew, ending the game. As I watched our seven-year-old Joseph droop in defeat and trudge off the soccer field—again—my empathy grew into a mountain.

I realized that this age was the time for learning the skills of soccer and practicing good sportsmanship, but I couldn't help questioning. Why was the other team always bigger, faster, and meaner than my son's team? Consistent defeat just didn't seem fair. After six games, the Pirates had not won once, and we were reaching the end of the season. It was difficult each Saturday watching Joseph play his heart out only to end in another miserable defeat.

One Saturday after another depressing loss, Joseph came up to me, put his hand in mine, looked into my eyes, and said, "Mom, would you pray with me that we will win our soccer game next Saturday? It's against the Footstompers—the best team in the league."

As I looked down at his greenish eyes, blonde hair, and sun-tanned face, I wanted to say to him, "Look, son. I graduated in physical education. I've coached basketball and softball, and I know quite a bit about soccer. You're on the worst team in the league; it's just the luck of the draw. It would be hopeless for us to pray for a victory for your team."

But I remembered Richard's softball. Had that been a logical prayer? Every morning our family got up, read the scriptures, and said our prayers. Joseph was holding my hand because of the dozens of times Hyrum and I had taught our children about the power of faith and prayer. As a family we had memorized Jesus' promise: "Ask, and it shall be given you; seek, and ye shall find; knock, and it shall be opened unto you" (Matthew 7:7).

Joe had accepted and believed these teachings. His request was now putting me to the test. Did I have the faith of my seven-year-old son? Could I put into action what I had been teaching my children?

I knelt down so that I could look straight into Joe's eyes and put my arms around him. "You bet, Joe," I said. "We're going to pray about this next game." His face lit up. It was the answer he had expected.

That evening at the dinner table, I explained to the family about Joseph's request and asked if we could include his desire in our individual and family prayers. Saturday came quickly, but we were ready. Joseph confidently dressed in his green Pirate uniform and the whole family jumped in the van to go cheer for him.

The coach had assessed Joseph's skills correctly and played him at center halfback position. He had an enormous "boot" and could kick the ball a long way, even as a small boy. Though the boys were taught during practices to play their field positions, this instruction seemed completely forgotten during the game. As the ball moved up and down the field, all the green Pirates and red Footstompers swarmed after it. Wherever the ball was kicked, they all ran toward it.

When Joe came off the field at halftime to rest and eat the traditional quartered oranges and get a drink, the score was 2–0 in favor of the Footstompers. From his position in the circle of tired players, he looked over at me with pleading eyes. As the coach finished his pep talk and the team broke up to return to the field, I walked over to Joe, put my arm around his shoulder, and whispered into his ear with a total confidence that came from deep within, "Joseph, somehow your team is going to win this game. You get out there, work your hardest, and do your very best, and somehow the Pirates will win."

As the second half began, the Pirates and Footstompers raced up and down the field, kicking the ball here and there, running after the ball in groups, and bumping into each other. Hyrum and I stood on the sidelines, cheering almost as loudly as Joseph's sisters, "Come on, Joe! Kick the ball! You can do it!"

All of a sudden, the Pirates had the ball in scoring position. A Footstomper fullback stopped the attack and began to dribble the ball over to the far sideline. As a Pirate forward went over to get the ball, the Footstomper had the good sense to kick it over to his own goalie, who could pick it up and boot it all the way downfield. However, the goalie wasn't paying attention; before he realized that the ball was coming toward him, it was too late. The ball rolled into the goal. One point for the Pirates.

Once again, the teams set up on the center line for the kickoff. After two or three minutes of running, kicking, and milling, the Pirates again found themselves on the Footstompers' goal line. As Footstompers battled to get the ball out and the Pirates battled to get it in, someone gave the ball a mighty kick. It ricocheted off the ankle of a little Pirate and spun across the goal line. The Pirate fans cheered wildly. The score was 2–2.

I was stunned. But as the teams positioned again for the kickoff, I glanced nervously at my watch. There wasn't much time left in the game. As the ball seesawed up and down the field, it was like an instant replay. The ball was moved down again into scoring position for Joe's team. The Footstompers' halfbacks and fullbacks fell back to form a wall of defense between the goalposts.

In my memory, the events that followed still have an ethereal quality. Joe was positioned in the center of the field, at the top of the penalty box. Out of nowhere, the ball rolled toward him. He stopped the ball and instinctively looked to pass or to defend the ball from any oncoming attackers. It took him a few seconds to realize that there were no attackers. Meanwhile, the Pirate fan club and particularly the Smith family were screaming from the sidelines, "Kick it, Joe! Kick it!" Joe looked at the goal, then at the ball, then at the goal again. Just as he realized that he had a direct shot at the goal, the defenders realized that no one was challenging him. As Joseph himself describes the slow-motion flurry of confusion, "it was like when Moses separated the waters of the Red Sea so the Hebrews could pass through."

All the green and red uniforms seemed to split apart and move to the sides, inviting Joe to kick the ball into the goal. Joe pulled his right foot back and booted the ball with all his might. It sailed right over the goalie's head and sank into the net. The Pirates had defeated the unbeaten Footstompers, 3–2! As the whistle blew, ending the game, Joe ran off the field into my arms. After accepting the congratulations of his jubilant teammates, family, and friends, Joe turned to me with a smile so big his eyes squinted almost shut. "Hey, Mom," he asked. "Can we pray that we'll win next week's game too?"

We taught our children the principle of prayer, but when it came to applying that principle, it seemed more often that they became the teachers. This was the case one summer afternoon in 1974. We had driven our Volkswagen van, with a pop-up camper trailer hooked to the back, from Portland to St. George to visit my family. With us were our five children—from Glenna, age six, down to baby Becca—plus Jason, our little dog, an important part of the family from the time we had acquired him as students in Provo, Utah.

On the return trip, we planned to head up to Yellowstone Park, further north to Banff, Canada, through Coeur d'Alene, Idaho, back into Oregon, and home. As we drove north toward Bear Lake, Idaho, we had to climb a steeply graded road through Logan Canyon. It was late afternoon and getting dark. We were anxious to find a good camping spot before night fell. I looked out the passenger window straight into the ravine below. It made me uncomfortable.

Just then, the van began to sputter and lag. Hyrum had just sufficient time before it died completely to pull over as close as he dared to the edge of the drop-off.

Now, Hyrum is a man of many talents, but auto mechanics is not one of them. We knew we were in trouble when he looked up front for the engine, forgetting that in a Volkswagen van the engine is in the back. Afraid of the steep slope, I kept the children in the van, telling them stories while Hyrum found the engine, stared at it, then tried to start it again. No response. He went back to the engine, looked again, kicked the back tire, then tried to start the van again. Nothing.

Finally, from the backseat, five-year-old Stacie piped up: "Why don't we pray, Dad? We've got to get where we're going."

Hyrum was fit to be tied at this point. I could see him literally grinding his teeth and knew he was repressing a snappish comment like, "Well, if you think it will work, Stacie, you just go right ahead and pray!"

But, being more mature, he humbly said, "Stacie, that's a good idea. Would you say the prayer?"

So we all bowed our heads, and Stacie earnestly explained: "Heavenly Father, our Volkswagen van won't go. We need to get to Bear Lake so we can camp and have a good night's rest so we can go on to Yellowstone Park tomorrow. So, Heavenly Father, would you fix the van?" Then she ended her prayer.

Dutifully, Hyrum turned the key. I saw the shock on his face as the motor promptly roared to faultless life. We pulled out onto the road and continued up the incline. I glanced into the backseat. Stacie, a satisfied expression on her face, smiled back if to say, "Why didn't we do that a long time ago?"

Our children's faith manifested itself in other ways as well. I marveled at their willing and cheerful obedience to our religious leaders. When the Church announced plans to build a temple in Seattle, all members who were assigned to that temple district, which included our family in Portland, were invited to contribute to its construction. As was our custom, we talked about it at a family council. Hyrum explained what money we had available through our investments and family savings, and the children reported on the status of their individual piggy banks and savings accounts. It wasn't much—just a thousand dollars—and it was literally all the spare cash we had. If we used it, we would leave ourselves without any savings. That might not have meant much to little children (Glenna, the oldest, was only seven), but they recognized it as a sacrifice. Without hesitation, they unanimously agreed that we should contribute that money to the temple fund.

We shouldn't have been surprised. A few months earlier, shortly after Becca's birth, I had gone to general conference in Salt Lake City with Hyrum. In one of the meetings, President Spencer W. Kimball asked members of the Church not to play games with face cards, since it might lead to gambling and other bad consequences. I was very troubled as we flew home. During those six months of pregnancy in bed, I had spent hours playing King's Corner with the children, using face cards for the game. Since it required a lot of addition and subtraction, I felt that it was educational, besides providing a pleasant family experience. The children loved the game. We had played it so often that we could recognize many of the cards from the back by their wrinkles and dog-eared corners. Yet the prophet's counsel was clear. Again, we brought up the subject at our family home evening. After we explained President Kimball's talk, we asked the children what they thought we should do. Glenna answered the question by getting up, taking the deck of cards, and dropping it in the wastebasket. I wept at the mighty faith of these little children.

In a way, I felt their faith was rewarded a few years later when we were serving on our mission in California. During that time, President Kimball visited southern California and attended a special meeting for all the mission presidents and their families. Prior to the meeting, the children were sitting in a spot from which they couldn't see the doorway. But they, like everyone else in the meeting, felt something special when this humble man—the living prophet of God—entered the room. As Glenna said afterward, "We knew when President Kimball came in the door, even though we couldn't see him."

The children's personal stake in following the prophet grew as they became older. As parents, Hyrum and I have been grateful for the clear guidelines of the Church on postponing dating until age sixteen. After a detailed discussion, we as a family committed to adopt this guideline.

The rule has been seen by our teenagers sometimes as a blessing, sometimes as a detriment. Some three weeks before Glenna's sixteenth birthday, she received a phone call from a boy who attended a different high school, inviting her to his junior prom. I heard Glenna say, "I'm sorry, but I haven't turned sixteen yet, and I'm not allowed to date." There was a silence, and then she said, "April twenty-fifth." Silence again for a longer period of time. Then, "Well, I'm sorry, but that's just the way it is." After Glenna had hung up she told me that she was grateful she had had an excuse not to go with him. He couldn't understand how two and a half weeks could make such a difference and had boldly stated so, offending her.

A few evenings later, Glenna was again called to the phone. This time her voice took on an animated sparkle. It was easy to tell that there was a special boy on the other end of the line. I was in the kitchen preparing dinner, but I could hear Glenna say, "Oh, I'd love to, but I can't. I'm not allowed to date until I'm sixteen. Could I have a raincheck?" I inconspicuously released the breath I had been holding.

After hanging up she told me, eyes aglow, that he had said he admired her for sticking to the rules and asked for the first date when she turned sixteen. I told her emotionally how proud I was of her for obeying the rule. Her reaction indicated that it had never occurred to her to do otherwise.

Incidentally, some time later the florist delivered a bouquet of sixteen roses from that young man. The card read, "Remember, when you turn sixteen, I have the first date." And he did.

The children's willingness to obey the prophet's counsel served our family well when in the fall of 1977 Hyrum was called as a mission president. We had always explained to them that a calling to one of us was a calling to everyone in the family, because everyone needed to support and sustain the person who had the responsibility. We would need their complete support in the months to come.

At ten o'clock one morning, the phone rang and a pleasant voice on the other end said, "This is President Romney's secretary in Salt Lake City. May I speak to Hyrum Smith, please?"

President Marion G. Romney was then the first counselor in the First Presidency. When I realized who was calling, I was so rattled that I gave the receptionist the telephone number of Hyrum's former office, a number that no longer worked, realizing what I'd done only after I hung up. She called back in a few minutes, and this time I managed to give her the right number. Hyrum was in a meeting but interrupted it to take the call. President Romney asked him if he would be willing to serve as a mission president and if I would support him. Hyrum said yes to both questions.

The timing, on the surface, looked terrible. We were at literally our lowest ebb financially. We had invested heavily in what we thought would be a growing company and had lost over a hundred thousand dollars. Worse, others who had invested blamed us, even though Hyrum had gone to each one beforehand and explained the risk.

We were on a stringent budget, building ourselves back from the edge of financial disaster. A mission is a full-time calling for three years. There was no way Hyrum could use that time to stabilize his business. The Church would provide living quarters and a modest living allowance for us, but there would be no extras. Who knew what the economy would be like when Hyrum was released from his calling?

And we didn't know where we would be serving. It could be anyplace in the world. What would we do about schooling for the children? So many things were building a foundation for the family in terms of music, athletic ability, and other talents. Would they be able to continue?

Hyrum was thirty-four. That was awfully young for a responsibility like this, even though I knew he was incredibly capable. His work in the stake presidency had proved that. But we both felt a great sense of inadequacy at the prospect of leading and motivating and nurturing more than 200 missionaries who would be under our jurisdiction. We had both served missions, not so long ago, it seemed, and our mission president and his wife had seemed so wise, so spiritually insightful, such examples to us. Could we be the same to our missionaries?

Still, there was absolutely no question in our minds that accepting this calling was the right thing to do. Hyrum owed his leadership abilities to the Lord; if the Lord needed those abilities in His service, then we were going to say yes. I had unwavering faith that the Lord would help us and take care of us, even though the way seemed mysterious to me. We never even considered saying no.

The hardest part was that we couldn't tell anyone about the calling until the new mission presidents were publicly announced a couple of months later. Of course, we shared the news with our immediate family, who were both pleased and supportive. Our children were really too little to realize what it all meant, but they were excited.

Even though we were willing to serve wherever we were sent, naturally, we were consumed with curiosity about where we would be assigned. Sometimes organized stakes are included within the mission's boundaries, but in some places, where the Latter-day Saint population is not sufficient to support stake programs, the mission supervises the local branches and districts. In such cases, missionaries frequently supply some of the ecclesiastical leadership while members are growing in numbers and expertise. Which would be our experience?

Then, in late February, the long-awaited assignment letter came.

My dad always helped me put in the garden every spring, and, by chance, he and my mom were there. We increased the anticipation by having a special dinner. I put the letter in a white sequined evening purse and laid it, with a fancy letter opener, on a little table covered with a special cloth. We talked about what it meant to accept a prophet's call. Hyrum and I expressed our joy and humility to our children. Then we all gathered around and, at our invitation, my mother opened the letter. We were called to the California Los Angeles Mission.

We were delighted! Southern California was well supplied with stakes and had five different missions at that point. Because of the strong local leadership, we would be able to concentrate strictly on working with nonmembers. We started making plans. Then a few weeks later we were informed that our assignment had been changed to the California Ventura Mission. At first we felt disappointed, but it turned out to be an enormous blessing to us. Los Angeles was then involved in a court-ordered busing program to desegregate its educational system. Our children would have been bused to four different schools had we gone there.

We had to be in the mission home on July 1. We worked like beavers all spring, grateful that we had no debts on appliances or furniture. We put our home on the market during an all-time-low national real estate slump. It sold the day we left for mission presidents' training sessions in Salt Lake City. We had a wall-to-wall house and garage sale. We sold our cars, every piece of furniture, and every personal item we could spare. Mother Ruth in Salt Lake City cared for the children while we joined with other mission presidents and their wives for a week's training. Thus began our new adventure. Glenna was ten and Becca was just turning four.

In a big way, the mission was an answer to prayer. We were together nonstop for three years, the only time in our marriage when that has happened. Hyrum began his day by helping get the children ready for school. Although he had all kinds of mission business (sometimes at all hours of the night) and was speaking every weekend, it was all where the children could see him and be with him. He could eat meals with us every day, and we could be with him every weekend, even if it was just to drive to a conference or a speaking assignment. It was a time of pulling together, of focusing on spiritual things, and of deepening our relationship with each other and with the Lord.

My fears about putting the children's lives on hold proved groundless. The house provided by the Church for the mission president was nicely furnished and in a pleasant neighborhood, so there were similarities with the home environment we had left in Portland. Ventura had wonderful youth programs in soccer, softball, basketball, and track, and we took full advantage of them. Joseph and Becca started playing soccer when they were four and five years old. All the children played basketball. What a thrill it was for them to have Hyrum consistently in the cheering section, usually accompanied by some of the missionaries. Surrounded by "big brothers" homesick for their own families, the children thrived.

We were also blessed to find a fabulous piano teacher, Connie Tice, a born-again Baptist with a strong personality and a great values system. The children performed in recitals almost monthly and had clear goals to reach. Their progress was exciting. The sixth-grade teacher loved chess and taught it to Glenna. She soon had the rest of the children excited about the game, and it became a family favorite. Mother Ruth even offered to help chaperone Glenna's sixth-grade chess team on their trip to a national tournament in Minneapolis, where they placed eighth in the nation.

We kept the mission rules scrupulously, and felt blessed for it. Our children saw the miracles that occur when people accept the Savior and find meaning in devoting their lives to him.

When we first arrived in the mission field, we had come with nothing but our clothes, our scriptures, ourselves, and Jason the dog. Three years later, as we prepared to leave the mission field, we were going with the same clothes, scriptures, ourselves, and our dog. We would literally be starting from scratch to find and establish a new home and career.

Yet we were laden with treasures—treasures that didn't require a suitcase in order to carry them. No suitcase in the world could hold the memories, the spiritual, cultural, and emotional growth, the soul- and mind-expanding knowledge, and the dear friends we had gained.

Dear friends, like Norm and Roberta in Portland, who took our nearly empty bank account and, over the three years we were gone, carefully invested and rebuilt it to an amount that allowed us some choices and got us started in the seminar business that eventually led to the Franklin Quest Company.

Dear friends, like Bob and Adele in Santa Barbara, California, who called four days before we left the mission field, apologizing at the thought of interrupting our well-earned month's vacation, asking if we could use some furniture. As Bob explained over the phone: "Six months ago our family with great reservations decided to sell our Palm Springs vacation home, and we did so. But when it was time to close on the house, the buying party could not come up with the money. Actually, our family was relieved and felt it was Providence's way of telling us the home wasn't to be sold."

This particular week our friends had gone to the Palm Springs home for a family vacation. While they were there, the previous buyers came to the door with money in hand, asking to buy the house. After a day of consultation the family decided to sell. The anxious buying party wanted to move into the house in two weeks, so all the furniture had to be removed as soon as possible.

Bob said apologetically, "It's secondhand furniture and a few years old. What money we would get by selling it to a secondhand store is nil, and we remember your telling us that you had sold all your furniture when you left Portland. Why don't you come see it and decide if you can use any of it?"

"Bob," Hyrum said, "we'll be at your house on the afternoon of

July first." That was the day we would be released and ready to leave Ventura.

When Bob and Adele showed us the furniture in their lovely Palm Springs home, the Smith family could do nothing but weep. From kitchen table and chairs to beds and bedding, sofas, lamps and end tables, washer and dryer—anything and everything we needed to set up a house and make it a home was there. It was a miracle.

I cannot tell this story even today without getting teary-eyed. At that moment we truly were wanderers, and the generosity of our friends brought us back to an earthly home.

In one little way the mission for me ended on what, given my particular loves and interests, was a great note. Part of my personal commitment had been to keep mission dress standards, which meant a dress every day for three years except on weekly preparation days. As a birthday present just four days before our release, my children (perhaps with some promptings from their father) gave me a new pair of Levi's, a shirt, a baseball hat, and tennis shoes. It was a great way to go on to the world we had left behind three years earlier.

In recounting the great blessings of our mission experience, I have not meant to imply that we were free from trials. Indeed, one of the most difficult spiritual struggles of my life began only a few weeks after we arrived in Ventura, when my mother was diagnosed as having ovarian cancer. The surgery was only partially successful, and the chemotherapy made her horribly sick. She stopped after two treatments because of her hair. Her hair had always been her crowning glory. She loved it. She loved taking care of it. She even loved taking care of my unruly mop, and my girls would sit still for hours as she curled their hair. She refused to let the cancer take her own hair away from her.

Mission rules were strict, and mission presidents and their families were discouraged from leaving their mission areas for any reason. Mom and I talked weekly on the phone, and she was cheerful and optimistic. "If John Wayne can beat the Big C, so can I," she would say. John Wayne was one of her most permanent heroes, perhaps to tease my dad, who couldn't stand him.

We fasted as a family for her. We prayed nonstop. Gallantly she researched alternative treatments, put herself on a healthy diet, and learned about a place in Greece that used an alternative treatment. My dad sold two acres of an alfalfa field, and she went to Greece in the spring of 1979, so weak she could hardly walk. She came back stronger and more cheerful. I slipped away for four wonderful days, bringing the children to spend Mother's Day with her. Mom seemed to be on the mend. But her doctor laughed. "Glenna, don't kid yourself. It's just a matter of time." His almost casual remark seemed to destroy the confidence and faith she had returned with, and although she kept up the diet and exercise, something seemed to break in her, and she started to slide downhill from that point.

My four sisters were all living in or near St. George. By telephone, I begged that we unite our faith and prayers in Mom's behalf. I felt that a miracle was needed, and that it would be a near certainty if we could simply make the necessary sacrifices. Surely the Lord would honor our request, especially since Hyrum and I had tried so hard to serve him faithfully and well on our mission. I felt so torn. Missionaries were asked to stay in the field, even if loved ones died, and I was a mission leader. I felt keenly the responsibility of setting a good example, but I wanted intensely to be with my mother. If I could just be there, maybe I could help rally her and the rest of the family. Finally, in November 1979, she called and asked if I could come home. She was starting to lose consciousness.

Hyrum could not leave, but I took Glenna Ruth with me and we left at four the next morning. I tried to prepare Glenna for the change that would have happened to her beloved Granny. I knew that Mom would be skeletal and only partially conscious. "If you need to come out to the van and cry, it's okay," I told her. Glenna did. Mom weighed only eighty pounds and was terribly weak. I could see her slipping away, and grief racked me. She had wanted to die at home, and my father rose heroically to the occasion, giving her her shots and taking care of her. I was grateful for that.

After several days, we had to get back to California. The day after we returned to Ventura, Dad called to say that Mom had died. I felt terrible to have been absent when she passed on.

Dealing with my grief was another ordeal. I had wrestled so hard for a blessing that she might be spared—now suddenly I felt empty. But it was a blessing that this loss occurred while I was serving a mission. Many insights had come to me because of the spiritual focus of our lives during that period. I understood better the sacrifice and commitment of my ancestors, to whom the death of loved ones was an everyday occurrence, whether on the trail to Utah or in the struggle to wrest a living from the harsh Dixie environment. I understood how death could be a sweet release in the context of faith in a loving Heavenly Father and a knowledge of the purpose of life.

Times of depletion come to everyone. Everyone suffers the death of loved ones, discouragements, disappointments, adversity, and sadness. The loving support of a united family is a great solace at such times, but often it is not enough to fill an inner emptiness. When I have felt depleted emotionally and spiritually—and it has happened often—my faith and conviction in God's love have kept me going.

In simple decisions, like donating vacation money to help build a new temple, as well as profound matters, like coping with the death of a loved one, the spiritual dimension of our family has always been an important foundation. Prayer to express gratitude to God and to seek his help has been a part of our relationship from the beginning to the present day. Hyrum and I have prayed for wisdom in every business decision, for understanding in every personal disappointment, for strength in every individual trial. We pray with and for our children. Family prayers at every meal and before every family meeting, and individual prayers as well, constantly weave an ongoing relationship with God.

Personal experiences like those shared on these pages are part of a family treasury of faith, a legacy of inestimable value. Like scriptural accounts of answered prayer, they become part of the collective "bank account" that any one of us can draw on when our personal faith gets shaky. They are reminders that if we will ask in faith, God will answer. They whisper to us that he is already listening. They rebuke our doubtfulness, correct our sloth, and encourage our gratitude.

These stories tell us the importance of attuning ourselves to the light within us so that the Spirit can speak to us without distraction or confusion. They tell our children that they are not alone. And perhaps most important, these stories are a witness that every human being belongs to a larger family where a loving Heavenly Father has room in his heart for all of us.

My roots lie deep

Traditions are a wonderful way for families to "hand down" treasured values. They are like heirlooms received from past generations, polished by the present generation, and passed on to the next generation. They create family closeness and joyful, enduring memories.

In organizing our year, we have consciously included traditions, associating times of the year with important family goals. Because traditions are often connected with holidays, they are special times that provide sparkle in our hard-working routines. I have been grateful that traditions were important to my parents, especially my mother. The love of family traditions was a vital part of her personal bequest to me. When I was growing up, every holiday had its own traditional events.

It was late September, too early for the cold weather to spread its crisp aroma around Dixie, but preparations for that wintry season began well in advance. One Saturday morning Dad harnessed up Old Nel and Tops, ready to pull the flatbed, rubber-tired wagon. Mama had lunch stored in the picnic box. The familiar gallon water jug, which my dad had meticulously fitted with a damp burlap gunnysack to keep the water cool, was fastened by leather thongs to the right front corner of the wagon. When my sisters and I were safely seated next to Mama and Dad on the wagon, my father

clucked at the horses and gave a flip of the reins. Thus we began
our journey to the river bottom to gather wood to keep our cook-
stove and fireplace aglow with snapping, lapping orange flames
through the winter.

As we bounced along the road to the river bottom, between
Dad's talking "Gees" and "Haws" to Old Nel and Tops, he told about
this year's spring floods, and how much driftwood they had left in
the bottoms. He reminded us that he and Mama would pick up the
long log poles and heavier tree stumps, and that our job was to
gather chunks of wood just the right length for the stove or fireplace. As usual, he ended his instructions with: "Oh, don't forget to
be on the lookout for this year's Christmas yule log. It has to be big,
fit in the fireplace perfectly, and be pitchie-pine. We want Santa
Claus to come to a warm house. Whoever locates the precise one
gets to hold the reins and help me drive the wagon back home."
During the remainder of the trip the conversation dwelt on the subject of Santa Claus and Christmas.

By the time we reached our destination, I don't know if it was
the competitive spirit (I would die for the reward of driving the
team of horses back home with my dad) or the Christmas spirit
tickling our stomachs that motivated us to work like the big Dixie
red ants hauling their winter stores to their nests. I do know that
between my sisters and me, we had our dad "come look" a jillion
times to see if this or that log was the precise one that would win
the prize. Just before the wagon was fully loaded with wood and
we were ready to head back home, Mama, as always, discovered
the perfect Christmas log. Even though Mama was the finder, Dad
always made us feel good about our day's efforts by letting each
of us take a turn at holding the reins and driving the team. Once
we got home and unloaded the wagon, the chosen Christmas log
was set in its sanctuary until the anointed eve.

As the autumn leaves began to fall from the mulberry trees
near the woodpile, the need for a fire in the fireplace would arise.
My job of gathering the kindling each night took me past the

Christmas log's waiting place. Some evenings, in moments of pro-
crastinating my job, I would walk over to the log, place one foot
on it, look down on its thick, gnarly, still shape, and think about
events to come.

On Christmas Eve, my father would take the yule log from its
shelter and carefully place it on a bed of kindling already prepared
on the fireplace grate. I used to imagine what Christmas Eve would
be like from the log's perspective. I imagined the log looking around
at its new surroundings in our fireplace, greeting a forest friend—a
tree dressed in her festive attire, with brightly wrapped gifts and
surprises tucked under and about her lowest boughs.

In my mind's eye, I could already see the Christmas log aglow
in the fireplace, casting light and warmth upon the family in the living room. There was Dad, sitting in his favorite chair, cracking and
eating roasted pine nuts and staring back at the flame. I could see
Mama soaking up the heat and wondering if she had remembered
everything she was planning to do to make this Christmas perfect. I
wondered if the Christmas log could see the anticipation on the
children's faces. Could it see me, or its own blazing reflection in the
gold and silver Christmas tree ornaments? Did it notice each carefully hung silver icicle, casting shimmering reflections of the flames
back at the fireplace? I imagined the log watching the Christmas
room through the Silent Night, lowering its flame just enough to let
Santa slip by to leave the hoped-for gifts and surprises. And then
when excitement chased away sleep in the household, the log
would continue to burn brightly while Christmas packages were
opened and Christmas wishes were granted. My reverie ended
when Mama called and reality set in. Darkness was always the
intruder, and I would go on about my unfinished chores.

Easter was another unforgettable time for family traditions.
Easter Sunday was generally reserved for contemplating the reality
and significance of Christ's resurrection. But the Saturday before
was the part of the Easter celebration most anticipated by a child.

On that day, my four sisters and I couldn't tumble outside fast enough to search the yard, the farm, and the outbuildings for our individualized Easter baskets. The baskets were never in obvious places, even when we were little. Through the years I found my Easter basket hanging on a branch in the almond tree, in the bottom of the irrigation ditch hidden under the thick ditchside grasses, in the haystack, and even in the thick growth of a rosebush. We sisters would help each other until the baskets were all found. In them would be boiled eggs that we had colored and marked with our names the night before, candies, jelly beans, and a little windup mechanical toy.

After we found our Easter baskets, Mama would send us on a treasure hunt. One particular year, I remember that the hunt started in a three-drawer dresser sitting at the side of the house. "Open the top drawer," Mama said. "There you'll find your first clue." There were strict ground rules about not reading a clue until everyone had arrived at the spot.

That first note sent us to the telephone pole down by the Jolleys' house. There we found a note that sent us another block away. This was no slouch of a treasure hunt! We went around blocks and up and down streets. We found clues on telephone poles, in mailboxes, in the crevices of house steps, in tree branches, and even in gopher holes. After a half hour, the last note sent us again to the chest of drawers where we had begun. There in the bottom drawer was a folded plastic shape that, when inflated, turned into a huge beach ball.

Later that afternoon, bringing the beach ball with us, we joined our extended family for an Easter picnic. Granny Wilkins brought the fried chicken. Aunts, uncles, and cousins all chipped in with food, balls and bats, picnic quilts, games, and more food. Mama brought her famous baked beans, another Easter tradition.

In addition to the extended family Easter picnic, other traditions came from my mother's side of the family. One unique tradition was the New Year's Jack. "Jack" was not a person, but a small gift—perhaps something that had been hidden away so well at Christmastime that Santa Claus had forgotten to deliver it. Or it might be something that had been wished for but that somehow had not shown up in the Christmas stocking. New Year's Jack was usually accompanied by candy, nuts, or fruit.

On Valentine's Day, we secretly placed carefully selected valentines on the doorsteps of neighbors and friends. We would knock on the door and then run and hide in nearby shrubs to watch until someone answered. We would remain hidden and quiet until the valentines had been discovered, discussed, and taken into the house. When the door was closed and darkness settled again, then and only then would we come out of hiding and move on to the next door to repeat the process. The evening of sharing love with others was filled with secrets, fun, and excitement.

With our own family, Hyrum and I have striven to continue, cultivate, and combine as many of these inherited family traditions as possible. Some have survived the generational transfer more or less intact; others have required adaptation to changed circumstances and living environments. While the specifics of some traditions have evolved as our children have grown, at the center of each a special core has remained. Excerpts from my journal detail two of our family's Easter adventures in 1979 and 1995.

April 14, 1979, Ventura, California

"Today we had our Easter fun. Hyrum got up with me at 5:00 A.M. We hid the Easter baskets in the front yard. The eggs we hid in the backyard, and the treasure hunt in the front yard. The children were ready to go at 6:45 A.M. We reminded them of the ground rules: keeping quiet when an egg was found that belonged to somebody else, and everyone staying together until the new treasure hunt clue had been read. They then hunted for their baskets, which were straw hats with jellybeans and candy eggs or rabbits in them. Then we moved to the back to hunt and found all the hard-boiled colored Easter eggs that we had prepared the night before. Then back to the front yard for the treasure hunt, with the first clue found in the rain drainpipe by the front of the garage, and the last clue ending the hunt in the garage with Becca and Joe so surprised, as were all the children, when they saw two baby Easter rabbits sitting in a rabbit house especially built for them. They were immediately named Nephi and Moroni. So all day we have played and loved Easter rabbits in the backyard."

April 15

"Sad day. One of the rabbits died. Stacie and Rebecca were really sad. We took the time to have funeral services for Moroni. We had a lesson on death and eternal life and read some scriptures on the subject. Hyrum dug a grave and we buried him in a Nike shoe box underneath the lemon tree. The kids made a headstone which said, 'MORONI our rabbit. Died April 15, 1979.'"

Here's a parallel Easter celebration, sixteen years later to the day:

April 15, 1995, Gunlock, Utah

"This year, in spite of the many directions my children have scattered, we were all together for Easter. Last night we had an electric time sitting around the kitchen table reminiscing and coloring Easter eggs. Their artwork and design has improved with age. Glenna and Ed [Glenna's husband] asked if they could set up the treasure hunt, in which I willingly acquiesced. All of the clues were in the form of nursery rhymes. For example: 'Little boy blue, come blow your _____.' We found the next clue in the mouthpiece of a small bugle hanging from the mantel above the fireplace. Another said: 'Little Miss Muffet sat on a tuffet, eating her _____ and _____.' That clue was found on a block of cheese in the refrigerator. We went from house to barn to haystack. One clue was even attached to the dog collar of our collie, Mac. The treasure was a

huge Easter basket filled with fruit, carrots, and flowers, instead of
the usual candy and chocolate eggs (it's interesting how even our
eating habits have changed over the years). There was also an aqua
plastic ball to take with us on our Easter picnic.

"Weather prevented our picnicking outside, so we decided to
make a big collage out of construction paper, showing things that
reminded us of Easter. Each of us did one item of our own choosing. It was agreed that we couldn't use scissors, but would have to
tear the paper to create the different shapes we wanted. We could
not use anything other than construction paper and glue.

"I made an Easter bonnet, with little cats glued around the
headband. Jacob made a shepherd and Sharwan created an Easter
egg. Each member of the family, including little Shilo, made something to contribute to the collage. Then Ed glued them all onto a
big sheet of poster paper and hung the finished product in front of
the fireplace for everyone to look at and admire for the rest of the
day."

The experience in making the collage was a first, the beginning
of a new family tradition. (Hyrum says that events become traditions when they are done for two years in a row.)

Another tradition that evolved in our family took place each
year on the first day of school. On that day, during our scripture
study time, Hyrum gave each of the children a father's blessing.
Then, after our morning routine was completed (on the first day of
school things always went without a hitch because everyone was
so excited about school starting), I would arrange the children
according to age and take a group portrait as well as an individual
picture of each child.

Then Hyrum would take over. He lined the children up on the
sidewalk in military fashion (he must have missed his Officer
Candidate School days). He would then shout: "ATTEN-SHUN!
Chins tucked in, shoulders straight, knees together!" He would check

their school apparel, making sure that "gig lines" of buttons were straight, shirts tucked in, and shoes clean.

Hyrum then gave them marching commands: "Left face! Right face! About face!" He would start giving the commands slowly and then increase the speed until the kids got all mixed up and burst out laughing. The "general" would straighten them out again and put them into a column, giving the "forward march!" command. "Left, right, left, right"—and off to school they would march. As they grew older, they became conscientious objectors, so the military maneuvers were dropped. But we always started the school year with the blessings, the photographs, and lots of hugs and kisses good-bye.

Although the yule log tradition I knew as a child is still part of our Christmas, we have embellished, invented, and added traditions until Christmastime is the king of our year. For the Smiths, Thanksgiving and the Christmas season are the culmination of the entire year, and the year-end traditions begin on Thanksgiving Day. While delicious smells are emanating from the kitchen, the family, extended family, and friends always play in the annual family "turkey bowl" football game—an event guaranteed to work up an appetite.

When at last all are seated around the table for Thanksgiving dinner, a kernel of corn is placed on every plate, a tradition Hyrum brought from his family. Each person in turn picks up his or her kernel of corn and expresses gratitude for the most important blessing received over the past year. It is a time of reflecting, sharing, and giving thanks, followed by the family prayer and the Thanksgiving meal.

The day after Thanksgiving officially begins the Christmas season, as we purchase and put up the Christmas tree. Each of us makes a special contribution to decorating the tree and house (inside and out). Hyrum puts the lights on the tree, Joseph puts up the creches, and Glenna builds a castle out of cardboard boxes and empty paper-towel and toilet-paper rolls, all wrapped in Christmas paper. Stacie arranges a Christmas scene on the piano, and Becca and Sharwan place the ornaments on the tree. Sharwan, being the tallest, does the top part of the tree and Becca the bottom. I put on the tinsel, a throwback to my own childhood. Jacob hangs up the Christmas calendar and places other Christmas essentials about the house. When all is completed, we turn off the lights and have a ceremonial lighting of the tree.

After the Christmas-tree lighting, Hyrum and I distribute to each child, according to age and needs, a precalculated amount of money. This money is to be used to buy clothes. The rules for clothes buying are:

1. Each person has to spend the money on clothes for himself or herself.

2. Any money left over has to come back to Mom and Dad.

3. After the satisfaction of making their purchases, they have to wrap each item individually and put it under the Christmas tree, to be opened and modeled on Christmas Day. This means that they have time in which to anticipate the pleasure of wearing their new clothes. And it also means that by Christmas we have the fun of packages of every shape and size piled underneath the tree.

We then have each member of the family make a prioritized "wish list" of items they'd like to receive for Christmas. Since the items have to be prioritized, the children are constantly making choices and balancing one against the other. For Christmas, Santa usually gets them their top one or two items, but he might also get them something totally unexpected—something they mentioned or wanted weeks earlier.

I remember Rebecca once eyeing and totally falling in love with a shiny, red, patent-leather telephone shaped like a high-heeled shoe. She oohed and ahhed and pledged slavery for one year if we would purchase the phone for her. At the time we said, "No way," and moved to the next store. Some months later I spotted the telephone in a catalog and ordered it for her for Christmas. I will never forget the excitement and exuberant burst of energy when Becca unwrapped that package.

Next, and most important in terms of the true spirit of Christmas, we send the family on a "research mission" to find an individual or family who needs special help. The following week, in our planning meeting, we decide together as a family whom we will help and how we might be of service to them. We hope that anything we do can be done in secret, anonymously. We have had some sweet experiences with this annual service project that brings the spirit of Christmas into each of our hearts.

Other traditions that we look forward to during the Christmas season include going caroling to our neighbors, friends, and extended family. We take a gift of home-baked bread, candy, or even souvenirs from places we have visited during the year. Another favorite tradition is to draw names the day after Thanksgiving so that each of us can become a secret "pixie" for another member of the family. Between then and Christmas we try to do good things and be of service to the person whose name we drew. On Christmas Day everyone guesses who his or her pixie was, even though most have figured it out already.

When the Christmas vacation officially begins and the family starts to gather home from school and work and travels, I set out a jigsaw puzzle on a card table where we can work on it piecemeal for several days. Everyone takes a hand putting it together when there's not something more urgent to do. The puzzle must be done by New Year's Day, when Hyrum glues it on a piece of cardboard to be saved.

Most of our activities reach their culmination on Christmas Day. On that most looked-forward-to of all mornings we get up around 7:00 A.M.—which amounts to sleeping in for the Smiths—and have a special activity before opening our gifts. One year, I found an empty barn and a manger on a country road, with no animals around anywhere. On Christmas morning we took the children to that barn and, standing in a cold and empty spot on the leftover straw, we read the Christmas story together. Away from the glamour of Christmas lights and pretty packages, the children gained a new perspective. At other times, we've climbed the hill above our town for our own Christmas service, reflecting on the true meaning of this sacred holiday.

Once we held our Christmas morning rendezvous at my dad's corrals on the river bottoms below Washington. He had always maintained them in the careful way a farmer must, but since his death in 1990 they had been neglected. Tumbleweeds had moved in to fill the empty spaces. The children, now in their teens or early adult years, easily saw the consequences of misuse and neglect, contrasted with our many pleasant memories of the area as a working part of the farm when Gramp and Granny were alive. Back at the house, we have a solid breakfast—after these early-morning expeditions, the appetite is never lacking. Then we get in our Christmas "line-up," from shortest to tallest, and take pictures. (It is interesting to review those pictures now and see how the children have changed places over the years.) In the living room we rekindle the Christmas yule log fire, sit down in our appointed places, and then open the gifts one at a time so that everyone can enjoy gifts of giving and gifts of receiving. Just as the yule log takes the night to burn, opening gifts takes the day, providing precious family bonding time.

It's popular these days for people to express concern about the materialism that has invaded much of the modern Christmas celebration, and I will be the first to agree that Christmas must always focus upon the Babe of Bethlehem and the gifts of life that he alone brought to each of us here on the earth. Our own experience is that Christmas, with Christ at the center of our thoughts, is a celebration of abundance—an abundance of love, an abundance of gratitude, *and* an abundance of gifts. In that order.

Hyrum has always said that learning is spaced repetition. Truly, the roots of traditions lie deep, but their branches must bear many leaves for the shadowfall to extend into the future. I know we're succeeding when a child says, "What will we do for our Christmas morning adventure this year?" or, "I have a perfect holiday puzzle for us to build," or, most important, "I have an idea for something we can do to help this family." Traditions truly are teachers of time-less values.

The shadowfall is long

It was early evening in Washington. I was sitting on the front steps, listening to the autumn chatter of sparrows in the old ash tree, when I spotted him. He tramped down the street, right past Misha's, not looking east or west as he reached the corner. Straight on, past Katie's house, he resolutely trudged directly toward me.

His worn western hat, pulled low over his eyes, forced him to lift his head so he could peer out from under the brim. The sliver of face exposed between the hat and his dusty beard was leathered brown. His long coat and baggy pants were oily, dusty, and full of patches and three-cornered tears that needed patches. The gunny-sack he packed over his left shoulder bulged with what appeared to be his only possessions.

I knew where he was headed even before he got there. Being a good watchman, I jumped up and raced to the kitchen to announce the arrival of yet another hobo.

Dad answered the knock at the kitchen door with his usual cheery welcome, then stepped outdoors to speak to the man. Five minutes later, I could hear the familiar repetitious thud of ax on wood outside and my mother's bustle with the kitchen pans inside. I knew that within the hour I would hear Mama's "yoo-hoo" out the kitchen door. The chopping sound would cease and my father would bring the hobo in, invite him to wash his hands at the kitchen sink, and usher him to a seat at our kitchen table for some of Mama's delicious cooking.

My dad had a way of making anyone and everyone feel at

home. After a few moments of uninterrupted silence at the table, broken only by the appreciative sounds of eating, the hobo would open up and tell us his story. My eyes and ears were always glued to our guest as he related tales of travel and adventure in places I had never heard of before. From the well-traveled men at our kitchen table I learned that there was no work in Iowa; that Atlanta, Georgia, offered no opportunities; and that sometimes it's just best to hop a train in Tennessee and head west. Sometimes I heard that the hobo was simply looking for winter work and thought California might be the place to go; usually he had a family and planned to send for them when he found a job.

The tramp's plate was slicked clean all too soon. Then my dad would walk to the door with him, offering our clean, covered haystack as a bed for the night. I don't recall any hobo ever taking Dad up on that offer; he always had a place to stay "up the road a ways" or "across the bridge." With a smile of appreciation and a full stomach, he would tramp off down the road again, leaving us with a neat pile of chopped wood.

It wasn't just hobos who found their way to our house. My dad, who often worked as a cook in the local cafe, seemed to attract all kinds of people who were "just down on their luck." Frequently, I would come home for supper to be introduced to a geology student from Pennsylvania or some such transient who was "passing through town when his car broke down and he didn't have enough money to fix it." If money was the problem, Dad got him a job washing dishes in the cafe and let him stay at our house until he could get back on the road. By working for what he got, the person could also feel some self-respect and was less likely to view himself as a "charity case."

My father, who was not in a position to assist these men financially, had a big, compassionate heart and could always find some way to help them out. I never did understand how the lines of communication worked in the culture of the less fortunate, but somehow the word spread that my house and my parents were good for a meal or a place to stay for any tramp or hobo traveling through the area who was willing to earn his keep. Dad quietly taught his children the golden rule, and that each and every person is worthwhile.

As my sisters and I grew up, we latched onto Dad's example. Between the four of us girls, we frequently had a friend staying at our house for one reason or another. Maybe her family was relocating and she needed a place to stay until the school year ended, or maybe things just weren't going so well at home. If it wasn't a friend, we took in a struggling relative or the relative's child who needed a home until the family could regroup, either financially or emotionally.

Dad's quiet example of compassion and assistance had a great impact on me as I grew up. One hot July I was home from college earning my next year's tuition by waitressing at the Liberty Cafe in St. George. One morning, a woman in her early thirties pushed through the cafe door and made her way to the counter. She plopped herself on a stool with a tired, heavy sigh, blew a fallen strand of hair from her eyes, and ordered an iced tea. As I brought her the cold drink, I couldn't help but ask her how things were going. Little did I realize that I had just poked a hole in a balloon filled with "hard luck," and it began to leak out.

Tired and on the verge of tears, she informed me that she was supposed to be in Colorado the next day to begin work at a summer youth camp. That morning, as she had been driving down the steep, narrow, winding highway that descends into St. George from the west, she had downshifted to slow the car, then heard a loud bang and lost all gears. With brakes as her only means of stopping, she struggled to bring the car to a halt while looking for a spot wide enough to pull over.

Knowing nothing about the mechanics of the car, she stepped out of the vehicle into the blistering desert air to wait for an empathetic motorist. About ten minutes later, a man and his young family pulled over to help. When the man realized that the car problem was more serious than he could handle, he offered to drive her into town. She felt uncomfortable leaving the car and her possessions unattended on the desert hill, so she asked the man if he would drive into town and arrange for a tow truck to come and get the car.

Some three hours later, the tow truck brought the woman and her vehicle into St. George. She learned that the car needed a new timing gear and it would take two or three days to order in the part and make the repair.

Taking one last, long drink of iced tea, she finished her story by saying that she needed to get over to the bank to arrange for money, she had to find a place to stay, and her car was full of dirty laundry she had planned on washing tonight in Colorado. She thanked me for the drink and for listening, then turned on the stool to leave.

Instinctively, my hand went to the pocket of my white Liberty Cafe uniform. I pulled out the keys to the blue 1949 Chevrolet that I called the Ben Franklin.

"Here," I said. "Take my car. I don't get off work until two o'clock. You can do your errands in that time."

She stared at me. "How can you do that? You don't even know me."

"What's your name?" I asked.

"Gloria."

"Well, Gloria," I went on, "it's not the greatest car, and it wouldn't make it all the way to Colorado, but it will get you around town. It's parked around back. Meet me here a little after two o'clock and bring your swimming suit. I'll take you along with the gang that will be waiting for me at home to the greatest swimming hole on earth. A cool swim on a hot day like this can sure make things look better."

She looked at me unbelievingly, slowly took the keys, and walked out the door.

After Gloria had left the cafe with the keys to my Ben Franklin,

I began to wonder about the wisdom of lending my car to a complete stranger. I called my mom to explain my spontaneous decision. Mom just laughed and told me to invite Gloria over for supper when she brought the car back. Hamburgers with ice-cold watermelon would taste good after our long swim.

And they did.

A fantastic payoff for Hyrum and me has been the willingness of our children to expend themselves in service at school, at church, and in the community. But there's nothing quite like the thrill of seeing second-generation personal giving—the direct, face-to-face generosity of a son or a daughter who feels such an abundance of time, talents, and love within that he or she can give it back.

Some twenty-five years after my experience with Gloria at the Liberty Cafe, I found myself at McCarran International Airport in Las Vegas, the closest major airport to St. George. In her last letter, Glenna had told us: "You will recognize him. He is as black as his teeth are white when he smiles. Please remember to be sensitive to the cultural differences."

As people continued to file down the ramp past us, I began to worry. What if he had missed the connection in New York? Maybe, among all these people, we had missed him. Maybe he was afraid and had chosen to be the last one off the seemingly packed airplane.

Glenna, Glenna! What have you done? I wondered. True, in the past we had had Makyla, Jack, Darby, Lance, Kyla—and the list goes on—stay with us for a season for one reason or another. But this situation was unusual, to say the least.

We had received the phone call in December: "Hello, this is the international operator with a collect call from Glenna Smith. Will you accept the charges?" Thoughts had raced through my mind as I wondered why our missionary daughter would be calling us from Italy. Missionary rules forbade calls except for Christmas, Mother's Day, and emergencies.

"Glenna, is anything wrong?"

Glenna's familiar and sorely missed chuckle answered us. She said, "No, Mom, but I do have a favor to ask of you and Dad. There is this missionary over here who will finish his mission at the end of November. He came to Italy two and a half years ago with a scholarship to attend a university in Rome. Two months later he met two of our missionaries and a short time later became a convert to the gospel of Jesus Christ."

Glenna went on to tell how the lifestyle and persecution of his roommates had forced him out of his apartment. At about that same time, the local mission president had asked him to serve a two-year mission for the Church, a calling he readily accepted. "When he finishes his mission he cannot go back to his home for fear of his life," Glenna said. "His country is in the midst of a civil war and political unrest. His hope since he joined the Church has been to get his education in America, at Brigham Young University, but he has no money and needs a sponsor to fulfill this dream."

"Okay, Glenna," I had responded. "What's his name and where is he from?"

There was a brief silence across the telephone line, and then, "Ogonggobah is his African name, but his English name is Vincent Musaalo and he is from Uganda."

At that point in the conversation, Hyrum, who had been listening in, at last spoke. "Glenna, this is a big undertaking."

"I know, Dad. That's why I already told him you would do it!"

Suddenly there emerged from the dark tunnel of the ramp a handsome young black man. He looked carefully around the room at the waiting groups of people. Finally he looked our way. A big smile broke out across his face. Glenna was right. There was no way we could have missed him.

Vincent is completing his undergraduate studies at BYU this year and is examining his options for graduate school. He hopes someday to return to Uganda and help his people there. Without

Glenna's readiness to help him solve his problems in Italy, a wonderful person and a brilliant mind might have been wasted.

Glenna is not alone among the children in picking up and carrying on the tradition of caring for and helping others. For example, Joseph during his junior or senior year in high school paid particular attention to a girl who was a little slow in learning due to a disability. He would enlist a couple of friends and bake a cake for her birthday, sing to her, single her out for congratulations when she participated in something, and make her feel special. Since this was a girl who was frequently overlooked by her peers, Joseph's kindness was especially meaningful. And Joseph never was too big or "too cool" to talk to younger boys, to ask how they were doing, or to encourage them. I know how much it meant to some of them.

Another example is Sharwan. Hyrum and I, along with Becca and Glenna, went to Argentina to pick her up in August 1993 at the end of her eighteen months of service as a missionary there.

We had strict instructions from Sharwan to bring all the boxes of T-shirts, socks, and clothes that the airline would let us carry. Everywhere we went, we distributed them. To find one home, we bumped down a long road to a rectangular adobe building where a family lived with no electricity or running water. Sharwan was as radiant as Christmas as she outfitted the whole family in the clothes we had brought. "She is our Evita," one member told us in labored English.

Sharwan insisted that we come with her to a little village near Viedma, where she had spent the last six months of her mission, so she could tell the branch members good-bye. A group of the young men of the branch, ages thirteen to seventeen, arranged a little party for her in the evening of the day we were there. We spent the day visiting and saying good-bye, then drove to the little chapel. Hanging outside was a huge banner that read, in Spanish: "Goodbye, Hermana Sharwan. We love you." Hyrum raised his eyebrows. The rule that missionaries use only their last names is just as strict now as it was when we were on our missions. Sharwan just grinned back at him, and he didn't say a word.

These people were visibly poor, yet somehow these seven or eight boys had pooled their pesos and collected some baked goods and sodas for refreshments. In their eyes was their adoration for Sharwan. She had encouraged them to stay active in that little branch, and they loved her. As each one came up and thanked her, I noticed that one of the boys was wearing a pair of her thick-soled, wide-toed, size-ten tracting shoes. I also recognized a pair of the thick hiking socks that she'd brought from home.

One of the people at the party was a full-time missionary from Utah who had been there for only a couple of months. He was the only one not snapping pictures, and Sharwan was aware of how tight his money situation was. She took the last picture in her camera, popped out the film, and handed him the camera. Hyrum and I looked at each other. Tears filled our eyes at her spontaneous generosity. I looked at her, literally empty-handed, and thought, *She's given away everything.* But I was wrong.

We left the party and went to a dinner with some other missionaries. In one of our last communications with Sharwan before we left for Argentina, she had asked Hyrum to host this last dinner with her companions so that the missionaries could save their always scarce funds for essentials. During and after the dinner, members and friends again came up to meet us and to tell Sharwan good-bye. As we got in the car to leave, Sharwan stopped. Here below the equator it was winter, and we were all wearing warm coats against the icy wind. Sharwan peeled hers off and wrapped it around a woman who had come to tell her good-bye.

As parents, we are excited to see our offspring choosing and using the values they were taught as children. Some would say that we were just lucky, that we happened to get good kids. I don't think it's explained that easily. Each of our children is very much his or her own person, but I believe that their adoption of and ongoing commitment to the values Hyrum and I feel so strongly about didn't just happen. And I don't believe that it was entirely a result of our Magic Three Hours, even though that process provided much-needed structure and gave us time for mutual learning and sharing.

As important as the structure and the shared responsibilities were, I believe that equally important were the many times when Hyrum and I took the opportunity to share with the children the stories contained in this book. Through that ongoing sharing was created a strong sense of our family's heritage, a feeling that our family—like every family—has its own special culture, and that the children have a part in that culture. Out of that awareness, the children have seemed to develop their own sense of responsibility to carry that heritage on into their own families and future generations. The stories of great-grandparents, grandparents, and parents, along with the shared experiences and memories of our own immediate family circle, have all helped our children feel that they are a vital link in an ongoing tradition that stretches back into antiquity as well as ahead into eternity.

This is not to say that the job of the transfer between the generations is complete, or that I can repose in my "mature tree" status and simply enjoy the shadowfall. But I do feel that much good for our family has come as a result of all that we have tried, both consciously and unconsciously, to share and pass on. I am especially interested in watching the beginnings of the transfer of values to the third generation. Stacie and her husband, Larry Shurtliff, have been carrying on many of our traditions in their little family, and a recent experience with their two-year-old daughter, Shilo, hints that the transfer is already beginning to take place.

The Smith 4, a singing group composed of Glenna, Stacie, Sharwan, and Becca, were performing in a Latter-day Saint meetinghouse in Vancouver, Washington. Shilo, having been taken out into the meetinghouse foyer so as not to disturb the others in attendance, charmed and befriended an older man who seemed a little uncomfortable about being there; he was waiting for his wife and daughter.

Shilo rolled a small ball she was playing with toward the man, and he retrieved it and rolled it back. They continued to roll the ball back and forth. Within a few minutes, Shilo and the man were having a wonderful time responding to each other. The man was smiling and seemed to be thoroughly enjoying himself.

Near the conclusion of the meeting, Shilo heard her mother and aunts singing the final song. Katie Fowler, Joe's fiancée, started to take Shilo through the door to hear the music, which was an arrangement of the Primary song "I Know Heavenly Father Loves Me." At the door, Shilo turned back toward the man in the foyer, beckoned, and said, "Come!" He got up and followed her inside, and together they stood at the back of the chapel while the song was sung.

Then it was time for the closing prayer. Shilo looked up at the man, folded her arms, and said, "Pray!" She made sure he folded his arms, and then she bowed her head while the prayer was offered. When Katie, who later told me this story, turned around at the conclusion of the prayer, she could see a tear coursing down the man's cheek. As the man turned to leave, Shilo leaned over from Katie's arms, reached her arms around the man, and gave him a hearty "Good-bye!"

The magic has begun again, a stem and a brief root shooting down. The shadowfall begins to appear, perhaps longer than I had expected.

15
Now I have heard

Weeks of preparation had gone into the evening's events. The round tables were set, each with a forest-green tablecloth and a burgundy, green, and navy blue floral arrangement, potted in brass. The wooden pillars supporting the large, roughly hewn crossbeams were wreathed with green ivy and strands of delicate white lights. The old prairie wagon, built by the Studebaker Company in the mid-1800s, stood against the wall, midway between the entrance and the reception line. The wagon, spiffied up to display Glenna's and Ed's wedding gifts tonight, was also ivy-covered, with a hand-made green and burgundy patchwork quilt draped over the driver's seat. Romantic, low lighting highlighted the rustic interior of Dixie's old Cotton Mill.

Glenna had chosen this site for her reception: the Rio Virgin Cotton Mill, located on Mill Creek in Washington, Utah, not far from the willows and arrow weeds I had played in as a child, where I first learned about God and faith. The mill had been built in the 1860s by my ancestors—the same ancestors who had planted the cottonwood and mulberry trees that shaded the special places of my childhood and youth. The old rock structure had been abandoned in my youth, and had provided us many hours of exploration and adventure. But tonight it glowed in its recently restored authentic grandeur.

My family, formally attired in dark burgundy or forest-green velvet, bartered for position in the reception line. Suddenly I was struck by the irony of it all. Tonight I had begged Hyrum, without succeeding, *not* to wear the black cowboy hat and silver hatband he had so carefully selected. I accused him of wanting to cover his balding head, but what I really meant was that the hat was inappropriate for the occasion. It just didn't go with his tuxedo.

Members of the old-timers band were setting up their equipment on the stage at the opposite end of the room, and the wedding guests were just beginning to trickle in. The band, also chosen by Glenna, was as historic—and rustic—as the building; it consisted of Quentin Nisson (of Abner's General Store) and his three sons. This seventy-six-year-old piano player had led the band that played at my own wedding reception, just three blocks east of where we now were. I couldn't help but reflect back on that night twenty-nine years ago.

One of the surprises of Hyrum's life had been our wedding reception. To Hyrum, a wedding reception meant standing in a line in formal dress, with candlelight glowing and soft music playing, while guests came through to pay their respects and to consume punch and cake before leaving. Hyrum had never been to a wedding reception in Washington, Utah.

To make sure everyone was invited, my parents and I had gone through the local telephone book. I could count on everyone in Washington being there; after all, a wedding was a major social event. After exchanging our wedding vows in a private ceremony in the nearby St. George Temple, Hyrum and I went that evening to the gymnasium of the old red-sandstone schoolhouse on Washington's town square for our reception.

There was a receiving line, to be sure, but that was just the beginning. In Hyrum's own words: "Everyone in the whole town came, left a gift, went through the line, sat down to eat, and then they stayed, and they stayed, and they stayed. There was a program and speeches, and Gail and I had to speak, and then they danced dances I'd never heard of"—schottische, Varsovienne, Spanish waltz, Virginia reel, rye waltz—"and then they danced some more. Gail and I were the first to leave our own reception."

As Hyrum stood by my side and greeted the proud townsfolk of Washington, many asked him how soon he and I would be moving back to Dixie. In each case, my city boy immediately responded, "I will bring Gail back to visit, but I will never, *ever* move to Dixie."

For the first twenty years of our marriage, Hyrum's work took him all over the country and required that we live in major urban centers where the action was. Coming back to Dixie was simply not an option. However, in the early 1980s, when my dad decided to sell several acres of the hay field I had tromped in as a youth, Hyrum and I purchased it. That decision was made more out of my sentiment than anything, but the seed was planted.

During the early years of Franklin Quest, we were both so involved in the company, and the children were so involved in school activities, that a move was not a realistic choice. Still, my ties to my Dixie roots were strong deep inside, and occasionally my old Virginian prayer would surface as a sigh, "Perhaps someday . . ."

By 1988, Glenna, Stacie, and Sharwan had all graduated from high school and had gone on to college in Cedar City, just fifty miles north of St. George. As Franklin had grown, I had moved out of active involvement in the company and was focusing again on the home front. Others were assisting in the day-to-day management of the company, relieving Hyrum of those former responsibilities, but he still maintained a heavy travel schedule, often traveling and teaching seminars from Tuesday through Friday. That was when I realized that it didn't matter where we lived as long as it was near an airport. This was enticing. Once again, a home among the sunny, sheltering red cliffs and lava-topped mesas of Dixie appeared to be possible.

As Hyrum likes to tell it, embellished for effect, I approached him with this proposition: "If I'm going to have to live alone anyway, let me live where I want to live." I reviewed my rationale: he could fly out of St. George almost as easily as Salt Lake City, and the children did not need to be tied to Centerville for school and activities as much as before. Hyrum agreed, and I started to plan for the move.

Once the decision was made, unexpected opportunities presented themselves. In the spring of 1988, our family went to visit my dad in St. George. On the day we were scheduled to return home, I went on my usual morning walk up into the red hills of Dixie, just north of my dad's house. On the way, I noticed a "For Sale" sign on a house; a sudden urge to walk down the long driveway to see the backyard overtook me. As I did so, I realized that this felt like the experience of meeting Elder Smith in the Thames van in London all over again. Sure enough—there was my garden space, fruit trees, a greenhouse, a basketball standard, a detached indoor sports court, a woodshed, even a swimming pool! I ran to Dad's house shouting at Hyrum with the exuberance of a four-year-old, "Come see, come see!"

We saw. Hyrum loved the house—but it lacked an office. I loved the yard and told him I would *make* his office. To my delight, we discovered that the original builders had planned to have an observatory room on the top floor and had built the staircase leading to it, but had later abandoned the project; the stairway led to nothing. It was the perfect spot for Hyrum's office. Before leaving St. George, we placed a deposit of earnest money on the home.

We sold our Centerville home and purchased an apartment in Salt Lake City so that Hyrum would have a home for the weeks when he wasn't traveling but had to attend meetings at Franklin's headquarters. The apartment would make it possible for us to spend part of our time with him on those occasions. In June 1989, after Joseph, Becca, and Jacob completed school for the year, we moved to St. George.

The move came at a good time for the three children still living at home. They quickly made new friends and found that there were even some advantages to being the new kids on the block. Joseph made the high school basketball team, as did Rebecca, who also found herself involved in the drama club, the volleyball team, and student government. Jacob found his niche in drama. These opportunities likely would never have happened in Centerville. Even though St. George had grown to be a respectable city of more than 30,000 people, it still retained a small-town feeling, and we soon were in the thick of community activities and events. I had returned to my roots, to the places that had shaped my spirit.

The Return of the Virginian

During the years that we lived away, Mama and Dad always kept three or four horses in the river bottom pastures for us to ride "when Hyrum brought Gail back to visit." And when we came to visit, we always seized the opportunity for a good horse ride. To my sorrow, less than one year after we moved to St. George, my beloved dad died of a heart attack and the horses were sold.

I finally suggested to Hyrum that it might be nice to have a horse or two of our own. I was delighted when he was very receptive to the idea, and occasionally on weekends we would take leisurely drives through the rural Dixie communities looking for horses or land that would be suitable for keeping them.

One day, as we were driving through LaVerkin, a small community about twenty miles up the river from St. George, we spied a sign advertising a pasture, barn, and corral for sale. We turned in to inquire. Hyrum stepped out of the car and was immediately drawn to a beautiful young stallion in the adjacent corral. He walked over to the fence, seemingly mesmerized. Later Hyrum described his experience: "That stallion was the most magnificent animal I had ever seen. Reddish-roan, huge, powerfully built. He held his head majestically, and stormed around the pen like he owned the place ... my kind of person."

Hyrum finally whirled around to me and exclaimed, "Gail, I've got to have this horse!"

I couldn't have been more surprised, and I found myself telling him that he didn't know what he was getting himself into. We had

no place to keep horses. He didn't know the first thing about own-
ing a stallion.

About that time, the owner of the horse sauntered out to see
what these awed intruders were doing at his corral. Hyrum's enthusiasm didn't wane even when the owner informed us that the stallion was only green-broke. Hyrum didn't seem to hear, or maybe
he didn't understand. "Is this horse for sale?" he demanded. I
crossed my fingers, hoping that it wasn't.

It *was* for sale, and Hyrum insisted on buying it.

I couldn't believe it. The Virginian was emerging! I immediately
felt an urgent need to ensure that he had a good experience with
his first cowboy acquisition. Knowing that when people start a new
venture at the top without learning the bottom, they can easily
become frustrated and discouraged, I casually (but desperately)
asked the owner if he knew of anyone who could help us with the
breaking and training of our new animal. I didn't realize it then, but
Providence had entered the picture again. A glimmer of my
Virginian had appeared, and this time it would not be extinguished.

The next morning I called the recommended horse trainer, John
Day, who owned the Rockin' D Ranch south of St. George. I told
John of my great desire that Hyrum have a good experience with
this horse. He agreed to pick up the stallion from the man in
LaVerkin and size the animal up.

Later, after he had checked out the stallion, he told Hyrum, "I
had to put a special kind of halter on your horse just to calm him
down. I put him in my trailer and he nearly kicked it apart as I
drove over to my corral. After three days, I didn't think I was going
to have any corrals standing." Then, with great earnestness, he said,
"You've got to get rid of this horse. It's going to kill somebody. Let
me help you find a horse more suitable for pleasure riding and
family ownership." Despite Hyrum's reluctance, he listened to the
counsel and we took John up on his offer. A few days later, John
notified us that he had exchanged the stallion for two horses.

Then John began teaching Hyrum how to ride. What I witnessed for the next six months can only be told in Hyrum's words:

"John started me out by putting me on the ground on my knees and hands, putting a saddle on my back. Then he got in the saddle and sat in it. He is a big man. He weighs 250 pounds.

"And he said, 'How does that feel?'

"I said, 'Well, that hurts.'

"He said, 'Well, that hurts the horse too.'

"Then John leaned over on my right shoulder, put all of his weight above my right hand on the ground, and said, 'Now lift your right hand.'

"I said, 'I can't lift my right hand when all your weight is on my right hand.'

"He said, 'Same problem with the horse. Everybody leans on the leg they want the horse to pick up. It makes it hard for the horse to do that. You need to lean on the other side and let the horse pick up the foot you want him to pick up.'

"Then he put the horse's bridle in my mouth, pulled back on it, and asked, 'How does that feel?'

"I said, 'That hurts a lot.'

"He said, 'Hurts the horse too. You don't ever have to jerk your horse's mouth around or it will get a hard mouth. If you treat your horse well, the horse will treat you well.'

"John drew the distinction: 'There is a difference between a cowboy and a horseman. A cowboy treats his horse like a hammer or a tool. A horseman treats his horse with respect.' It totally changed how I related to a horse. John Day taught me how to be confident on a horse."

We now had two horses, and Hyrum surprised me for my June birthday with a beautiful palomino mare named "B." We pastured our horses on my uncle Denny Cooper's property in Washington. Our son Joseph and Stacie's husband, Larry, spent the summer erecting a large prefabricated hay and horse shelter that we promptly dubbed the Taj Mahal.

Benjamin Franklin once wrote wisely about the true cost of a major purchase: "When you have bought one 'fine thing,' you must buy ten more, that your appearance may be all of a piece." We learned for ourselves the truth of what Franklin had written. The horses were indeed "fine things," and we soon found that to own and use them we had to buy saddles, bridles, blankets, brushes, a watering trough, horse trailer, and feed. But I began to see a new side of Hyrum revealed through the love he obviously felt for our new animals.

The ultimate "fine thing" arising out of the purchase of our new horses manifested itself a few months later. Hyrum and I were visiting with Mark Walters, the real estate agent with whom we had worked to purchase our St. George home. On his desk, along with some papers, was a photograph of a beautiful ranch, with green fields, a river running through it, an attractive ranch house, and other outbuildings, all nestled in a scenic valley. I pointed to the photo and said, "Mark, if you ever find a ranch like that for sale, we'd be interested." To our surprise, he told us that the owner of that particular ranch had come into his office that very morning and asked Mark to sell his ranch for him. Before the day was over, we had driven to the Turtle Mountain Ranch, located near the scenic little village of Gunlock, about twenty-five miles northwest of St. George. Within months, we had purchased the ranch—a "fine thing" to house the horses.

Hyrum and I are very different people. Hyrum's a sprinter. I'm a long-distance runner. His enthusiasm is like a rocket, throwing off sparks even on the launch pad. I ask questions, collect information, and make plans; he marches off and does a thing immediately. We've learned to trust these different styles in each other; as a result, we're a better team and make better decisions than we would otherwise.

If I had to characterize myself, I would use the symbol of a clock. I've always had a love affair with old clocks. Great-grandmother Averett's clock, given to my dad, sat on the mantel above the fireplace and tick-tocked faithfully all the years of my childhood. During our first year of marriage, while we were stationed in Germany in the military, I entered an old furniture shop to look for a piano and fell in love with a wall clock, dust covered and plain faced in a black box. It was leaning against the wall, upside down, as if it hadn't been touched for years.

For five dollars it was mine. I pulled it out of its hiding place, took it home, cleaned it, and hung it on the wall. It always reminds me of the beginning of our marriage. After we got it back to the United States, I put the ceramic bride and groom from the top of our wedding cake on the floor of the clock's pendulum case, with the gold pendulum swinging behind. I love the steady swing, the steady tick-tock, the steady movement through time. To me, the old clock ticks consistency into all our lives.

Hyrum, on the other hand, has always loved eagles. Displayed around our home are various paintings and photos of eagles. A large bronze statue of an eagle swooping to land on a gnarled branch is the first thing that greets visitors as they enter our front hallway. A painting of a eagle adorns Hyrum's office at Franklin Quest, and several of the prized mementos and awards displayed on his office walls have eagles as motifs. To Hyrum the eagle symbolizes keen vision, powerful wings, strength, high goals, speed, endurance—the attributes of leadership and achievement.

Thus when we finally purchased the Turtle Mountain Ranch, we promptly renamed it the Eagle Mountain Ranch. It's an appropriate name, not only because of Hyrum's love of eagles, but also because several golden eagles nest in the rugged cliffs just below the ranch house. It is indeed a beautiful place, situated along the cottonwood-lined Santa Clara River and surrounded by hills covered with juniper and pinyon pine. At an elevation nearly a thousand feet higher than St. George, the ranch is significantly cooler than town, especially during the hot Dixie summers.

The ranch has turned out to be one of Hyrum's great joys, one that he fully shares with the entire family and numerous dear friends. It is a place of refuge from hectic travel schedules and the pressures of being a chairman of the board and chief executive officer. Many a weekend we spend in the rustic ranch house, with its two-story stone fireplace and displays of historic firearms, eagles, clocks, and western art on the log walls. The windows of our ranch bedroom open out on the horse pastures, and I'm still a little surprised when I look out and see Hyrum—the city boy who would earlier have shunned such a life—talking with the nuzzling horses.

Equally amazing to me is the transformation in dress. Hyrum, who before would never have considered being seen in public in anything but a suit, spends much of his time at home and on the ranch in cowboy boots, a western shirt, Levi's with a big belt buckle, and, for outdoors, a Stetson.

The first of several hundred guests approached the reception line, bringing me back to Glenna's wedding evening. Hyrum had succumbed to my pressure and had placed his hat on the windowsill behind him. "Well, you're back in Dixie, Hyrum. I knew you'd bring Gail home," said a local old-timer, with a countrified handshake and pat on the back. Our next few guests said basically the same thing. *Poor Hyrum,* I thought, *you're in for a long night.* Then the comments seemed to cease. I looked up at Hyrum. He had put his black cowboy hat with the silver band back on. The hat was doing the speaking: "I'm back! Yes, I've brought your Dixie girl home. I've got the red sand between my toes, and I too seek the shade of the cottonwood tree." Behold the Virginian.

In silent moments since that night I have wondered when the change really began in Hyrum—until last Christmas. Hyrum's younger sister Pauline gave him a photo she had found in an album of their mother's. Enclosed in an antique oval frame was a picture of Hyrum when he was about eight years old. He is decked out in a black cowboy hat, shirt, vest, big-buckled belt, white scarf, and gun and holster—but no boots. He's even wearing a pair of cowboy chaps, each leg emblazoned with the names "Roy Rogers and Trigger" (my childhood heros!) and a depiction of Roy on a rearing Trigger. It was my Virginian in embryo, speaking to me down through the decades: "Shucks, ma'am, it only took me forty years to find my boots."

Epilogue: Long upon an afternoon

When Hyrum first gave me the gift, I did not particularly care for it. Although the print was elegantly framed, the scene was depressing to me. I was young, I had small children, circumstances were happy, and I did not want to be reminded that there was a sad side to life. It was a thoughtful gift, and I hung it on the hallway wall of our house in Centerville. In time, though, I quietly removed it from the wall and stored it in the closet until another day.

That day came some nine years later. Hyrum and I were furnishing and decorating our newly purchased ranch house in Gunlock, Utah, using all the household keepsakes that could never be thrown away and had therefore been stored for "another day." Coming upon the nearly forgotten print, Hyrum pounded a nail in one of the logs of the wall, took the picture out of the box, and hung it on the wall. My reaction to the scene was different this time. My earthly journey had produced scars that taught me the meaning of the message depicted by the artist.

The painting depicts the experience of the Martin handcart company. Some of the Mormon pioneers were so poor that they carried their few belongings across the plains in wooden, two-wheeled handcarts. During the summer and fall of 1856, five handcart companies pushed and pulled their frail vehicles from the Missouri River all the way to Salt Lake City. Three of the companies reached the valley without major difficulties, but two had been delayed in their departure and were overtaken by an early winter as they struggled along the Sweetwater River valley in the highlands of what is now central Wyoming. The Martin handcart company, the last to depart from the East, suffered most severely when trapped by the early snows.

The painting shows a pioneer mother huddled with an older daughter, both wrapped in shawls and tattered blankets, carrying a bundled-up infant. Buffeted by wind-driven snow, a little group watches as two men lay the frozen body of the women's spouse and father to rest in a shallow grave scraped from the icy earth. In the near distance, a cold and still loved one from another wagon is being carried in a blanket to be buried in the same grave. As the wind whips the snow around the onlookers, wagons can be seen in the background ready to move on as soon as the brief ceremony is over. There is no time for grief. Survival dictates that the pioneers move on.

My pioneer ancestors could not have endured all that they did merely on some vague hope that there was a better world beyond the harsh and dangerous and unforgiving one in which they lived. As I have read of their experiences, especially those accounts that have come down in their own words, I have seen that they did not merely hope. They *knew*. In my youthful experience among the arrow weeds of the creek bottom below Washington, I too came to know something of what they knew, and I felt that knowledge grow within me over the intervening years as I experienced the loss of my grandparents, my mother, my father, and my youngest sister, Nola.

I am thankful that such events are unforeseen, for, as it turns out, those earlier experiences were stepping-stones to the tragedy that wrenched our family in May 1995. This time I was the woman in the painting. I stood with my husband and many others in the little pioneer cemetery at Gunlock, not far from our ranch. We all huddled together to observe the burial of our daughter Sharwan and our granddaughter, little Shilo Sharwan. The rains fell in mourning, but umbrellas kept us dry. In the background the scene revealed automobiles that were prepared to move on as soon as the ceremony was concluded. Unlike the handcart pioneers, we were not forced to move on in order to survive physically; our comfortable homes were only a short distance away. Yet the same knowledge and inner understanding of eternal principles possessed by my ancestors demanded that I move on emotionally and spiritually.

I do not want to leave the impression that moving on is easy. It is desperately difficult. My mind keeps going back to the day of the accident. Thoughts run through my head over and over, repeating all the "what-if" scenarios in a vain attempt to change the day. My heart aches with the thought of their earthly absence from our family. But in reality I have to ask myself, what changes could have been made?

I had been in Salt Lake City taking care of Shilo while the Smith 4 were taking care of some preparations for their scheduled performances at the governor's ball and the Utah Summer Games. That morning I had adhered to my normal Magic Three Hours routine of arising early, reading the scriptures (John, chapter 15), and exercising for an hour. Sharwan had accompanied me to the swimming pool of our apartment complex.

The Smith 4's morning schedule required last-minute fittings and alterations for their costumes. Before they left for their appointments, we all knelt in family prayer. When we finished, there was a special closeness among us. We gave each other hugs, and the girls departed. During the hour my daughters were gone, I enjoyed taking care of Shilo. Being her granny was a role I cherished.

It was about 10:30 A.M. when the girls returned from their errands. Excitement filled the room as they chattered about the costumes and upcoming events. In the same store where the alterations on the dresses were being made, Sharwan had found a bridal veil that she loved, so she had purchased it on the spot. She placed it on her head and asked me how I liked it.

"Pretty great," I said.

Typically, Sharwan retorted, "Oh, Mom, what do you *really* think?"

I hesitantly reassured her of its beauty. The hesitance came because, as I saw her standing there in the veil, I felt the twinge of her leaving the nest, and June 24 was not that far away. I'm sure that every mother feels such a tug at the heart prior to her daughter's marriage.

Soon the focus changed to preparing Sharwan, Stacie, and Shilo for the drive back to St. George. They needed to be in Gunlock by 5:30 P.M., so that Sharwan could judge a rodeo queen contest and Stacie could accompany one of the contestants on the piano.

Sharwan disappeared with Shilo, then reappeared a few minutes later with a bathed bundle wrapped in a bath towel. "I want to be an angel girl," Shilo said.

With that plea, Sharwan stood her on the large bay-window ledge, put the towel around Shilo's back so she could grasp the corners of the towel, extend both arms out, and spread the towel like the wings of an angel. This had become an after-bath ritual for Shilo. Then she pulled the towel down around her and snuggled in its fluff.

The twelve o'clock departure time came too soon. Sharwan was holding the elevator door open. I was taking my last-minute hugs and kisses from Shilo and giving last-minute travel counsel to seven-month-pregnant Stacie, when Shilo spotted Sharwan waiting for her in the elevator. She ran to the waiting arms of her aunt, shouting, "Let's go, Wannie!" Everyone else hurried onto the elevator and the doors closed.

Around 3:30 P.M. I looked at my watch and calculated about where they would be on the interstate highway running from Salt Lake City to St. George. I figured that they would be approaching Parowan, with about an hour remaining before they reached St. George. They would also be within the range of cellular phone service at Cedar City, so I called Wannie on the car phone. Yes, she replied, they were near Parowan. They had stopped a few minutes earlier at McDonald's in Beaver. Sharwan told me she had called the bridal dress shop and made all the arrangements to pick up her wedding dress. I could hear Shilo's laughter and chatter in the background. The sounds made me say to Sharwan, "Take good care of my babies."

Wannie answered back, "Oh, Mom, you know I'll take the best care of them."

Fifteen minutes later Stacie's husband, Larry, called me on his cellular phone. "Gail, there has been an accident with Stacie and Sharwan."

My first question was, "Has anyone been hurt?"

Larry replied, "I don't know. 1 was talking to Stacie on the cellular phone when I heard her say, 'Sharwan! Sharwan!' and the phone went dead. I tried to get her back on the phone but there was no answer. So I called 911 to report what I thought might be an accident. Someone had already reported it, and they told me the car was registered to Hyrum and Gail Smith. They would not give me any information other than come to the Cedar City hospital emergency room as soon as possible."

Glenna, Becca, and I fell on our knees and prayed to God for the courage and strength to be able to handle whatever had happened. I called Hyrum, who was on his way to the office, on his car phone to alert him of the accident. He immediately returned to the apartment.

Imagination controls the mind at times like this. The feeling of somehow knowing, yet not knowing, that something is seriously wrong. The hope of a miracle that somehow all will be right. It was long upon an afternoon before the details came of the unexplained one-car rollover, the passing of Sharwan and Shilo, and the miracle of Stacie and her unborn baby, both of whom survived.

I have never tried to live without faith in God. I have never wanted to. I believe that faith is a real thing, as real as what we see and touch and hear and taste. The things of the physical world can be understood by the evidence of the physical senses and the more precise methodologies developed by scientists. But I believe, in an age when too many look to the physical world for the only explanations of our existence, that a surprising number of us sense deep within that there is also a spiritual dimension to life. I believe that this spiritual dimension can be understood only by the spiritual senses, senses that each human being is born with, but that too many of us rationalize away or overlook as we get older.

Only those who have experienced what I have in these past weeks will understand the depth of my own sorrow and how much I miss my daughter and granddaughter. But through it all has come an underlying feeling of peace, which I sense is the "peace that passeth all understanding" of which Jesus spoke. That peace is the spiritual assurance that this life really is but a way station in a longer journey that reaches far back before our birth and extends forward into eternity.

In the words of a favorite Mormon children's hymn, "Families can be together forever, through Heavenly Father's plan." Seen in this perspective, Sharwan and Shilo, while plucked away from our family, have only passed to the next stage of eternal existence. Although we cannot see or associate with them now, I rest in the assurance that they are once again with their loving Father and with Mama and Dad, Papa and Mother Ruth, and others who have gone before. And, most important, I know that Hyrum and I, along with Glenna, Larry and Stacie, Joseph, Becca, and Jacob, will all be together face-to-face with Sharwan and Shilo at some future day when we have ourselves passed through death's doorway. When that happens, we will realize that our separation was for but a brief moment.

As I have pondered the events of May 18, 1995, and the events following the accident, I have been and continue to be overwhelmed at the outpouring of love and support from family and friends numbering in the thousands. I understand more than I ever have about the nature of faith, about miracles and eternal matters, and about sensing their reality deep within and trusting in them.

I understand now more than ever the power of parenting. Although Shilo's stay in this world was brief, she had the vision of eternities because everything she saw was good.

As for Sharwan—for several weeks I had been struggling, trying to achieve some feeling of closure so that I could emotionally and spiritually begin to move on. On a quiet Sunday morning, in a moment of grieving, I climbed the stairs of our St. George home to our Eagle Room, with its large windows looking over Dixie. As I sat down, pondering and pining about the loss, through my tears I saw Sharwan's day planner lying on top of the desk. Intuitively I unzipped it and began paging through it.

Every page was neat and orderly. Her journal was caught up to the day she died, her checkbook current and accurate. There were neatly typed pages of uplifting quotes, poems, and stories, as well as photos of family and friends she held dear.

Tears brimmed anew as I found an encouraging letter I had written to her six years earlier. "Keep those brown eyes sparkling," it read in part. "Remember that when the road gets rough, we put our trust in God and figure out an inspired solution. What you are supposed to be in earth life—leave that in God's hands. He'll use you where you are needed most, and when it comes along, the Spirit will confirm." She had carried that letter with her constantly from the day she received it, and I had never known.

But the healing comfort for which I yearned came as I turned to a beautiful photograph of the six spires of the Salt Lake Temple silhouetted against a backdrop of planets, stars, and galaxies. It was a glimpse of the eternities, the realms of order, beauty, and peace. Again tears welled up in my eyes, and I rose from my chair and walked to the window. Through watery eyes, I saw the morning sun glistening on the tender spring leaves of the century-old ash, mulberry, and cottonwood trees. Their sturdy trunks faithfully supported the profusion of branches, limbs, stems, and leaves all reaching out and up to touch the blueness of the sky. The morning shadowfall from these magnificent trees was cast westerly, with shaded limbs and leaves awaiting their turn in the sun.

Peace touched my heart like a presence. My daughter knew who she was and what she was about. The values and treasures transplanted into her life had struck their own roots and sprung up high and strong. She was casting her own giant shadowfall beyond the veil. To this parent, that was the most magical feeling of all.

Standing at the window, I marveled at the land marked by shadowfall, brightening westward into a perfect day.

Index